Gabriele Esposito

Armies Across History no. 4

French Colonial Troops 1815–1914

Organization, uniforms and weapons

STRATUS

Published in Poland in 2024
by STRATUS sp.j.
ul. Żeromskiego 6A,
27-600 Sandomierz, Poland

as
MMPBooks,
3 Gloucester Close,
Petersfield
Hampshire GU32 3AX, UK
e-mail: office@mmpbooks.biz

http://www.mmpbooks.biz

ISBN
978-83-67227-52-0

Editor in chief
Roger Wallsgrove

Editorial Team
Bartłomiej Belcarz
Robert Pęczkowski
Arthur Juszczak

Cover
Artur Juszczak

DTP:
Stratus sp. j.

PRINTED IN POLAND

Table of contents

The Army of Africa, 1830–1914 3
Chronology of the Army of Africa's campaigns 5
The Zouaves 8
The Tirailleurs 25
The Chasseurs d'Afrique 38
The Spahis 54
The Bataillons d'infanterie légère d'Afrique 65
The Saharan units 68
The Tunisian and Moroccan native units 71
The Naval and Colonial Troops, 1815–1914 75
The Native Troops, 1815–1914 88
Select bibliography 112

About the author

Gabriele Esposito is a military historian who works as a freelance author and researcher for some of the most important publishing houses in the military history sector. In particular, he is an expert specializing in uniforms: his interests and expertise range from the ancient civilizations to modern post-colonial conflicts. During recent years he has conducted and published research on the military history of the Latin American countries, with special attention on the War of the Triple Alliance and the War of the Pacific. He is among the leading experts on the military history of the Italian Wars of Unification and the Spanish Carlist Wars. His books and essays are published on a regular basis by Osprey Publishing, Pen & Sword, Winged Hussar Publishing and Libreria Editrice Goriziana; he is also the author of numerous military history articles appearing in specialized magazines like *Ancient Warfare Magazine*, *Medieval Warfare Magazine*, *The Armourer*, *History of War*, *Guerres et Histoire*, *Focus Storia* and *Focus Storia Wars*.

The Army of Africa, 1830–1914

The French *Armée d'Afrique* or "Army of Africa" has been without doubt one of the most iconic military forces in the history of the world. The great quality of its units and the elegance of its uniforms, in fact, are well known around the globe and are a fundamental component of France's glorious military past. The Army of Africa has participated in all the major wars fought by France during the period 1830–1962, giving a major contribution from an operational point of view; it has been an elite component of the French Army for more than a century and has influenced military fashions around the globe for long time. The units that made up the *Armée d'Afrique* had a distinctive colonial character, since they were created to operate in French North Africa; they consisted of corps recruited from French personnel as well as of locally-recruited corps having French superior officers (in which local elements could be commissioned up to the rank of captain). From a formal point of view, however, the Army of Africa was not a separate component of the French military forces but an autonomous component of the metropolitan French Army. French North Africa, in fact, was not administered like a normal colonial territory by the French government, due to its proximity to France. As a result, the denomination *Armée d'Afrique* was an unofficial one that was used to identify the French military units serving in North Africa; it was not an official denomination indicating a separate branch of the French military forces. It became increasingly popular after 1873, when the whole French Army was reorganized in 21 army corps after the disasters of the Franco-Prussian War. The military corps stationed in North Africa were re-structured as the XIX Army Corps. The latter, in fact, was commonly known as *Armée d'Afrique* due to the fact that it was the only army corps of the French Army whose military district did not cover mainland France. All the other overseas territories of France were garrisoned by military units that were not part of the metropolitan army but of the *Armée Coloniale* or Colonial Army, which could trace its origins back to the second half of the 17th century and which was controlled by the Ministry of the Navy. As a result of the above, the *Armée d'Afrique* was an autonomous branch of the metropolitan French Army and thus controlled by the Ministry of War. In addition to the famous Foreign Legion, the Army of Africa comprised four main categories of units that will be analysed in the present work: *Zouaves*, *Chasseurs d'Afrique*, *Tirailleurs* and *Spahis*. In addition to these, this text will also cover the lesser known *Bataillons d'infanterie légère d'Afrique* (commonly known as *Bat'd'Af*), the *Compagnies méharistes sahariennes* and the semi-regular *Goumiers*. Until 1881 the "native" corps of the Army of Africa were recruited only from Algeria; with the French occupation of Tunisia of that year, however, new units made up of Tunisian soldiers were added to the existing ones. Later, starting from 1908, the transformation of Morocco into a French protectorate led to the creation of new Moroccan military corps inside the ever-expanding *Armée d'Afrique*. From an ethnic point of view the Army of Africa comprised Arab, Berber and French individuals; the latter could come from metropolitan France or be – especially after the first decades of colonization – French settlers living in North Africa (known as *Pieds-Noirs*). Until May 1913 no form of conscription existed in French North Africa and thus all the native soldiers of the *Armée d'Afrique* were volunteers; the French individuals, instead, could be conscripts or volunteers. All the various components of the Army of Africa developed a strong military identity soon after their creation and adopted distinctive uniforms that were admired across the world for their style. The *Zouaves*' dress, for example, became so popular around the second half of the 19th century that it was copied by several armies of the time from Europe to the Americas.

The Romantic ideals of the first half of the 19th century played a major role in influencing the early character of the *Armée d'Afrique*: beginning with Napoleon's Egyptian Campaign, in fact, the elite classes of the European states had started to love exotic cultures like the Arab one of the Middle East or the Moorish one of North Africa. This cultural phenomenon – known as "Orientalism" – became dominant in all the arts; France was greatly affected by it and thus changed her perception of the Islamic world. The Kingdom of France, after the glorious days of the Napoleonic Period, was in search of a new political identity and wanted to restore – as soon as possible – its previous status of military power. The French Army, after some years of stagnation, was gradually re-building its previous international position and was in search of new opportunities to show its potential. The exotic world of North Africa, inhabited by peoples of mixed culture and surrounded by a veil of mystery, started to attract French colonialists but also French society in general: a country like Algeria, in fact, was perceived as a "land of opportunities" by many in Europe. The French had no clear idea of the Algerian natural resources, but were strongly determined to play an increasingly important role in the politics of the Mediterranean area. For centuries Algeria had been dominated by the so-called "Barbary pirates", who operated across the western portion of the Mediterranean Sea and who raided the coastline of southern Europe quite frequently. From a formal point of view, the country was part of the Ottoman Empire; the latter, however, entered a phase of great political and military decay during the 18th century and thus – in practice – ceased to exert a proper influence over Algerian lands. The Turkish presence, consisting of a few merchants and of some small military garrisons, was felt only in the major coastal cities; the immense interior areas of Algeria, in fact, were mostly inhabited by nomadic tribes that were fully independent from Ottoman control.

The Muslim pirates of North Africa had been a pain in the neck for the Europeans for more than two centuries: initially their actions had been sponsored by the Ottomans, but with the progression of time they had become autonomous from the political will of the latter. As a result, especially after it became clear that the Turks were in no conditions to defend their territories in North Africa, the European powers started to have a more aggressive behaviour towards the Barbary pirates. During 1801–1805 the naval forces of the young United States fought against the Muslim pirates in the Mediterranean, obtaining some significant victories; in 1816 an Anglo-Dutch fleet bombarded Algiers with the objective of putting an end to the slave trade that still existed in North Africa. These events showed to the world that peace and order in the southern Mediterranean Sea could be restored only with a European occupation Algeria. The latter country was officially known as the "Regency of Algiers" and was ruled by a governor known as a "dey"; this person, appointed by the Ottoman sultan, exercised effective control only in and around Algiers since the rest of the country was governed in an autonomous way by provincial governors known as "beyliks". These had strong links with the local communities and effectively controlled the military potential of Algeria. The two beyliks of Oran (located to the west of Algiers) and of Constantine (located to the east of Algiers) were the most powerful ones. South of the coastal provinces of Algiers, Oran and Constantine there were the lands inhabited by the nomadic Berber tribes; these lands were part of the immense Sahara Desert and were characterized by an extreme climate that was quite different from the Mediterranean one of northern Algeria. To the west of the Regency of Algiers there was the Sultanate of Morocco, an independent Muslim state that had never been conquered by the Ottomans and which had been a major military power of Africa for long time. To the east of Algeria, instead, there was the Ottoman "Beylikate of Tunis"; this, like the Regency of Algiers, was ruled independently from the Ottoman Empire albeit being formally part of it. Most of the interior areas of Algeria had never been explored or visited by the Turks, whose military presence in the country consisted of a few Janissaries who made up the small garrison of Algiers. The Algerian governors were rich and powerful thanks to the profits that came to them from the slave trade and from the actions of the pirates.

The so-called "Barbary Coast" – comprising also Tunisia and Libya in addition to Algeria – was a real naval power in the Mediterranean Sea. The agile Muslim warships moving from North Africa attacked undefended Christian cargoes along the major sea routes and captured substantial quantities of valuable goods; they also raided Christian coastal settlements in search of slaves, who were later sold into the markets of North Africa. Some minor European states, like the Kingdom of Naples, were forced to pay a yearly tribute to the Dey of Algiers in order to protect their ships and coastline from the attacks of the pirates. The Kingdom of France suffered from the actions of the Barbary pirates like all the other Christian countries of the Mediterranean; until 1827, however, the French government never considered the possibility of invading North Africa to eradicate the problem represented by the sea-raiders. Charles X, being at the head of the restored Bourbon monarchy, was in search of an opportunity to increase his popularity. He was not particularly beloved by his people despite having done his best to increase France's political importance on the international scene. In 1823 an army of 100,000 French soldiers had marched into Spain, with the objective of crushing the local liberals and of restoring absolutism. In 1828 a smaller expeditionary corps had been sent to southern Greece, to support the Greeks in their war of independence against the Ottomans. Both these campaigns, however, won no territories for the Kingdom of France and saw no glorious victories for the French Army. As a result, by 1830, Charles X was in search of a "*casus belli*" thanks to which his government could intervene in Algeria.

In 1795–1796 the French Republic had purchased large quantities of wheat for its army from two Jewish merchants who were active in Algiers. These had debts with the Dey of Algiers and did not pay them for several years. When the two merchants were forced to pay their debts by the Algerian authorities, they refused to do so by claiming that they had never been paid by the French government for the wheat purchased during 1795–1796. In 1820 the French consul in Algiers, Pierre Deval, was ordered to solve this problem by Charles X but made no provisions to pay the merchants. Several years passed without seeing any progress and thus the diplomatic relations existing between France and Algeria worsened. On 29 April 1827 Deval had a meeting with the Dey of Algiers, during which the latter struck him with his fly-whisk after a hot-tempered discussion. Charles X soon used this offence made to his diplomatic representative as a mean to increase pressure over the Algerians. He initiated a naval blockade of the port of Algiers that lasted for three years and that caused serious economic damage to the Algerian merchants. The blockade, however, did not stop the raids of the Barbary pirates and also had very negative consequences for the merchants of southern France who could no longer export their products to Algeria. In 1829 the French tried to resume negotiations with the Dey of Algiers, but the latter responded with cannon fire directed towards the French blockading warships. Following these events, in the spring of 1830, an armada of 600 French ships was assembled in the port of Toulon together with an expeditionary corps of 34,000 soldiers for the occupation of Algiers. The French conquest of North Africa was a very complex political and military process that lasted until 1903; for reasons of space, it will be summarized in the detailed "Chronology" that follows. This will not comprise the campaigns fought by the Army of Africa outside North Africa, which will be covered in the histories of the various military units.

Chronology of the Army of Africa's campaigns

- **14 June 1830:** Following a plan made by Napoleon in 1808, General de Bourmont lands with his expeditionary force 27 kilometres west of Algiers – at Sidi Ferruch – without meeting resistance. After the landing of the French, the Dey of Algiers starts assembling an army to stop the invaders. In a few days he is able to mobilize 7,000 Janissaries taken from Algiers' garrison, 19,000 local soldiers recruited by the Beys of Oran and Constantine and 17,000 warlike Berbers of the Kabyle tribes.
- **19 June 1830:** The Algerian military forces are defeated by the French on the open field at the Battle of Staouéli, after suffering severe losses.
- **5 July 1830:** The French troops enter Algiers after just three weeks of campaigning in North Africa. The Dey capitulates in exchange for his personal freedom and for the possibility to retain possession of his personal wealth; on 10 July he leaves Algiers and goes into exile at Naples with his own family. The Ottoman Empire accepts the loss of Algeria and thus the surviving Janissaries leave North Africa for Turkey.
- **July–August 1830:** The French – despite having agreed to preserve the liberties, properties and religious freedom of Algiers' inhabitants – start plundering the city and desecrating religious sites. Meanwhile, a few days after the news of Algiers' capture reaches France, Charles X is deposed by his own people as a result of the so-called "July Revolution". His cousin Louis-Philippe, nicknamed the "citizen king", is called to preside over the new French constitutional monarchy. The new Liberal government formed after the revolution is not interested in expanding the conquests made in Algeria, but the victories of the French Army in North Africa are already enormously popular in Paris. General Bourmont, a supporter of Charles X, abandons the Algerian city of Oran that had already been occupied with the idea of returning to France with part of his troops to restore the absolute monarchy. After encountering strong opposition to his plans from the officers under his command, Bourmont resigns and goes into exile in Spain. Louis-Philippe chooses General Clauzel as new overall commander of the French military forces in Algeria.
- **September–December 1830:** The local Algerian governor of Titteri, a city located not far from Algiers, tries to coordinate his military efforts with the Beys of Oran and Constantine to stop the French penetration into Algeria. Due to their internal political divisions, however, the Algerians are defeated by a column of 8,000 French soldiers (commanded by Clauzel) at Mèdéa in November. Meanwhile the French try to occupy the important city of Blida, but are prevented from doing so by the strong resistance of the local Berber tribes.
- **1831–1833:** Clauzel establishes a civil administration in Algiers and starts recruiting local soldiers with the objective of stabilizing the French presence in Algeria. A company to acquire agricultural land and to distribute it to settlers coming from France is created, with the objective of transforming the Mitidja Plain (located south of Algiers) into an area for the intensive production of cotton. An increasing number of French military officers and civilian administrators become interested in expanding the French territories in Algeria. Meanwhile the French authorities start to exert a certain political influence over the Beys of Oran and Constantine, who continue resisting against foreign penetration with the decisive support of the Kabyle tribes. Despite suffering some minor defeats, the French are able to occupy the city of Oran in 1833.
- **1834–1836:** The Algerian territories are formally annexed to the Kingdom of France, together with their Muslim population of 2,000,000, as a military colony. The latter is ruled by a governor having both civilian and military authority, including the power of executive degree. Despite encountering strong resistance from the Berber tribes, the French troops are gradually able to conquer most of the Mitidja Plain. Meanwhile, in the province of Oran, the young Abd al-Qādir emerges as a prominent leader of the resistance forces. The latter were strongly determined to fight a *jihad* or "holy war" against the foreign invaders. Abd al-Qādir rapidly assumed control over most of western Algeria, gathering an army with thousands of fighters. In 1835 a first major engagement is fought between the French and Abd al-Qādir near the Sig River; despite suffering heavy losses, however, neither side can claim victory. The campaign continued with the retreat of the French, who were later attacked and routed by the Algerians at the Battle of Macta. The French authorities were thus forced to send more troops against Abd al-Qādir, under command of the experienced General Bugeaud (a veteran of the Napoleonic Wars and an expert in irregular warfare). In July 1836 the Algerians are defeated by Bugeaud at the Battle of Sikkak. Abd al-Qādir decides to continue fighting against the French only with guerrilla methods. In the east of Algeria the Bey of Constantine continues his resistance against the foreign invaders, but in November 1836 his territory is invaded by a French force with 8,700 men under command of Clausel. The latter is defeated at the Battle of Constantine and is forced to resign.
- **1837–1843:** After some successful Kabyle raids against the settlements of their newly-arrived colonists, the French decide to mount an offensive against the Berber tribes living around their territories. The Zwawa Kabyles, the strongest tribal group of northern Algeria, are progressively defeated after putting up a strong resistance. During 1837, after a very difficult siege, the French are finally able to occupy the city of Constantine. Meanwhile General Bugeaud

concludes the so-called Treaty of Tafna with Abd al-Qādir, according to which the latter is recognized as the overlord of most of Algeria's interior areas. The great Algerian warlord used the treaty signed with the French to consolidate his political power over the various Berber tribes. In 1839 hostilities between Abd al-Qādir and the French resumed: the Algerians initiated a full-scale "holy war" and attacked the foreign settlements in the Mitidja Plain. Abd al-Qādir's offensive is crushed at the Battle of Oued El Alleug, but most of the French farms are pillaged or destroyed. In 1840 Bugeaud assumes command of the military forces fighting against the Algerians and institutes a new strategy that combines scorched earth tactics with the use of fast-moving cavalry columns tasked with intercepting the highly-mobile enemy contingents. In 1843 Abd al-Qādir's own camp is raided by the French and 5,000 of his men are captured. After this defeat the Algerian warlord is forced to retreat into the Sultanate of Morocco.

- **1844:** Abd al-Qādir is able to conclude a treaty of alliance with the Sultan of Morocco, who feared that the French could also attack his realm after invading western Algeria. Since the later months of 1843 the French troops had already started chasing the Algerian fighters deep into Moroccan territory and this had increased tension between France and Morocco in a significant way. On 6 August 1844 the Franco-Moroccan War officially began with a French naval bombardment of Tangiers. A few days later, on 14 August, the decisive Battle of Isly takes place between the Moroccan Army and the French military forces commanded by Bugeaud. Despite numbering 25,000 against 11,000 French, the Moroccans are defeated decisively. Following this serious defeat and the French storming of the coastal city of Mogador (16 August), the Sultan of Morocco agrees to sign the Treaty of Tangiers with the French. According to the latter, Morocco accepts establishment of a well-defined border with French Algeria and to stop supporting Abd al-Qādir in his rebellion against the French.
- **1845–1847:** Abd al-Qādir continues his resistance against the French, but now has to also fight against the Moroccan troops. Abandoned by the Berbers of western Algeria, he is finally forced to surrender on 21 December 1847. Meanwhile the French conduct an effective campaign against the Zwawa Kabyles, forcing them to surrender after many years of raids and skirmishes.
- **1854–1857:** After some years of relative peace, the Kabyle tribes revolt again against the French under the leadership of a charismatic woman named Lalla Fatma N'Soumer. The rebellion is finally crushed by the French, albeit with some difficulties.
- **1871–1872:** Algeria, now having a civil administration after the fall of Napoleon III's Second Empire, is shattered by the so-called "Mokrani Revolt". The latter saw the participation of more than 250 tribal groups from all the provinces of Algeria, led by Cheikh Mokrani (a warlord of the Kabyles living in the Biban Mountains). Taking advantage of the ongoing Franco-Prussian War, the Berbers mounted a large-scale rebellion that also affected the Army of Africa with the mutiny of some units that had been ordered to go to France in order to fight against the Prussians. The insurgents attacked several French settlements and killed many colonists, exerting their control over a large portion of Algeria. After some weeks of initial difficulties, however, the Army of Africa was able to react and to mobilize a total of 22,000 soldiers. On 22 April 1871 the rebel troops, which were marching against Algiers, are defeated at the Battle of Boudouaou and are forced to fall back. A few days later 20 columns of French soldiers started to reconquer the Algerian interior areas, intercepting the major groups of rebels. On 13 July 1871, following their victory at the Battle of Icheriden, the French were able to capture most of Cheikh Mokrani's relatives. By the early months of 1872 order had been restored in Algeria.
- **1881:** Following the Congress of Berlin of 1878, which had defined the spheres of political influence of the European colonial powers in Africa, France decides to occupy the Beylikate of Tunis. The latter, albeit being formally part of the Ottoman Empire, was ruled as an autonomous country since 1830. On 28 April a French expeditionary corps with 28,000 men, commanded by General Forgemol de Bostquénard, entered Tunisia; after conquering Bizerte, the French moved on Tunis and occupied it on 3 May. Being unable to put up a proper military resistance, the Bey decided to surrender and to sign the Bardo Treaty. The latter transformed Tunisia into a French protectorate and thus its signing was followed by a general insurrection of the Tunisian people. The latter, however, was soon crushed after the French Navy bombarded the coastal city of Sfax and a French expeditionary corps with 32,000 soldiers was landed at Kairouan. By the end of 1881 Tunisia had been officially annexed to the French colonial possessions in North Africa. During 1881 a first French military expedition was sent to south-eastern Sahara, with orders to conquer the Hoggar Mountains. This unit, however, was annihilated by the Tuaregs (the warlike nomads living in southern Algeria).
- **1882–1901:** The French penetration into the vast and unexplored lands of southern Algeria continues, albeit being slowed down by the elusive combat tactics employed by the Tuaregs. Despite encountering serious difficulties, however, the French were progressively able to occupy the western regions of the Touat, the Gourara and the Tidikeit. During this same period the French built the famous Trans-Saharan railroad and established a new border between Morocco and Algeria. After consolidating its positions in southern Algeria, the French government decided to colonize the vast desert area located between North Africa and Senegal.
- **1902–1903:** The Tuaregs of the Hoggar Mountains are defeated by the French at the Battle of Tit. Meanwhile the French government launches a series of minor military campaigns in order to occupy the desert regions located south of Oran and bordering with Morocco. On 17 August 1903 the nomads of south-western Algeria and south-eastern Morocco are defeated by the French at the Battle of Taghit. The French occupation of Saharan Algeria is officially completed.
- **1907:** Émile Mauchamp, a French doctor living in Morocco, is assassinated by a mob in Marrakesh. This incident is used by the French government as a "*casus belli*" for intervening in Morocco. The city of Oujda, located on the border between Morocco and Algeria, is occupied in March; in August, the city of Casablanca is bombarded by the French.

- **1908–1910:** Without officially declaring war on the Sultanate of Morocco, France continues to send military contingents across the Algerian border and reaches the Ziz River (located 200 miles within the national territory of Morocco). Taking advantage of the chaotic political situation existing in the Sultanate, the French military forces occupy most of south-eastern Morocco without encountering strong resistance.
- **21 May 1911:** France occupies the important Moroccan city of Fez, a significant step towards the transformation of Morocco into a French protectorate. Germany reacts to the French expansionist moves by provoking the so-called "Agadir Crisis", which ends with a victory of the Anglo-French diplomacy.
- **30 March 1912:** The Sultan of Morocco signs the Treaty of Fez, according to which his country becomes a French protectorate. The signing of the treaty is followed by the outbreak of several popular uprisings, which are crushed by the French with great difficulty.
- **May 1912:** Moroccan insurgent forces attack the French garrison of Fez, but are repulsed after suffering severe losses.
- **September 1912:** The most important military contingent of the Moroccan insurgents is defeated by the French troops at the Battle of Sidi Bou Othman. Following this clash, the city of Marrakesh is occupied by France and the first pacification of Morocco is completed.

Map of Maghreb, the region of Northern Africa comprising the French colonies of Algeria, Tunisia and Morocco from which the units of the Army of Africa were raised.

The Zouaves

History and organization

Soon after the occupation of Algiers in 1830, General Bourmont had to face two main problems. Firstly he had to find a way to garrison the newly-conquered territories without counting on the units that had made up the expeditionary corps, since most of the latter were going back to France; secondly, he had to demobilize the defeated military forces of the Regency of Algiers without causing an outbreak of native uprisings. The possible solution to these two problems was to form some native auxiliary corps recruited from the former Ottoman soldiers, which could help the French in garrisoning Algiers. General Clauzel, the successor of Bourmont, realized this project by ordering – on 1st October 1830 – the creation of a first unit of native infantry. The members of the new corps soon became known as "Zouaves", from the name of the Kabyle "Zwawa" tribes from which they were recruited. The Zwawa communities, living in Algeria and in Tunisia, had always provided excellent soldiers to the Ottomans and thus had a well-established military tradition. The new Zouave Corps initially had just four companies, which were soon expanded to eight. Before the organization of the first unit could be completed, however, on 21 December 1830 Clauzel decided to expand the Zouaves to two battalions with eight companies each. The early years of the Zouaves were characterized by great difficulties, since their desertion rates were extremely high and thus the French experienced great problems in keeping the two battalions alive. In order to reach the planned establishments an increasing number of French volunteers had to be admitted into the Zouaves' ranks. Initially only the officers and NCOs of the two battalions had been French, but by 1833 a third of the rankers were not Algerian. Many French soldiers

Private of the Zouave Corps (left) and volunteer of the "Volontaires Parisiens" (right) in 1831. ASKB

who were part of the garrison left in Algiers volunteered to become Zouaves, asin the latter corps discipline was not so strict and a ranker had more opportunities to become corporal or sergeant. In addition, the French volunteers were greatly attracted by the magnificent uniforms of the Zouaves. These, in "Moorish style", consisted of an "idealized" version of the Zwawa communities' tribal dress that was heavily influenced by the Romantic aesthetic ideals of the time.

In 1831, to complete the organization of the two battalions, the French authorities were even obliged to recruit some inexperienced volunteers coming from Paris. These, organized into a volunteer corps known as *Volontaires Parisiens*, were former revolutionaries who had fought against Charles X in July 1830 and who were sent to Algeria after the end of the revolution. On 7 March 1833 the Zouaves officially became a *corps mixte*, i.e. a military corps made up of local recruits and of French volunteers. The two existing battalions were disbanded in order to form a single battalion with ten companies. Two of the latter were entirely made up of French volunteers, while the remaining eight had 62 Algerian and 12 French soldiers each. In 1835 the 2nd Battalion of Zouaves was formed, being followed by the 3rd Battalion of Zouaves in 1837. The recruiting problems experienced during the previous years, however, continued to exist since the number of Algerians wishing to serve in the corps remained very limited. On 4 August 1839 the 3rd Battalion of Zouaves was disbanded due to the lack of new recruits, but it was re-raised after just eight months. On 8 September 1841 the three existing battalions were assembled together into a single regiment and thus received a more stable structure. The internal establishment of each battalion was increased to eight active companies and one depot company. Two months after the Zouaves' reorganization, the new *Tirailleurs* were created. Since the latter consisted entirely of Algerians, the number of native soldiers in the Zouave regiment started to decrease very rapidly. Initially the 8th Company of each battalion continued to be made up of local recruits, but by 1848 there were no more Algerians in the Zouave Regiment (which officially ceased to be a *corps mixte* in 1849). With the reorganization of 1841–1842 the Zouaves started to include a certain number of conscripts, but this always remained quite limited since the flow of volunteers wishing to serve in their ranks remained significant.

On 13 February 1852 Napoleon III ordered a general expansion of the Zouaves, in which the corps was re-structured in three regiments with three battalions each. The existing three units became the first battalions of the three new regiments and the internal organization of the single battalions did not change. With the reform of 1852 the Zouaves also received a proper light infantry status, since until that moment they had mostly acted as line infantrymen. They had, for example, replaced their drummers with trumpeters. In April 1854, following the outbreak of the Crimean War, the Zouaves were called for the first time in their history to serve outside North Africa. Each of the three regiments was asked to provide two *Bataillons de Marche*, i.e. temporary units created to serve overseas for the duration of a conflict. The six temporary battalions, having eight companies each, were formed with the best elements

Native officer of the Zouave Corps (left) and NCO of the French Royal Guard in campaign dress (right). The early Zouave Corps included cadres provided by the French Royal Guard. ASKB

Drummer (left) and French officer (right) of the Zouave Battalion in the early 1830s. ASKB

Native private (left) and French NCO (right) of the Zouave Battalion in the early 1830s. Note the different colour of the turban. ASKB

Soldiers of the Zouave Battalion patrolling the streets of an Algerian city in the early 1830s. ASKB

from each regiment and were assembled together into three temporary regiments with two battalions each. The battalions of the 1st Regiment were assigned to the 1st Division of General Canrobert, the battalions of the 2nd Regiment were assigned to the 3rd Division of General Bonaparte and the battalions of the 3rd Regiment were assigned to the 2nd Division of General Bosquet. During the Crimean War the Zouaves fought with incredible courage and with great determination, winning the admiration of Napoleon III as well as of their enemies. At the Battle of the Alma (20 September 1854) the battalions of the 3rd Regiment of Zouaves launched a surprise attack against the Russians after advancing on some broken terrain, captured the enemy guns and using them against the Russians. Following this incredible action, a magnificent statue representing a Zouave was placed under the newly re-named Alma Bridge in Paris and Napoleon III decided to raise a new Zouave regiment for his recently-formed Imperial Guard. The Regiment of Zouaves of the Imperial Guard was formed on 23 December 1854 and was to consist of two battalions with seven companies each. The new corps was recruited in Crimea, from the best elements of the Zouaves and of the metropolitan light infantry who were already fighting against the Russians. Meanwhile the Zouaves continued to distinguish themselves during the combat operations, especially at the Battle of Balaklava (25 October 1854) and at the Battle of Inkerman (5 November 1854). Now including the Zouaves of the Imperial Guard, they also played a prominent role during the decisive Battle of Malakoff (7 September 1855).

The years of the Second Empire saw the Zouaves taking part in France's most important military campaigns. In 1859 the four regiments all participated to the Second Italian War of Independence, fought against the Austrians. They were reorganized as follows: the regiment of the Imperial Guard reduced the number of companies in its battalions from seven to six, the other three were expanded to four battalions each (three active and one of depot), with six companies in the active battalions and three companies in the depot battalion. For the Italian campaign the 1st Regiment was assigned to the 1st Army Corps, the 2nd Regiment to the 2nd Army Corps and the 3rd Regiment to the 5th Army Corps. The Zouaves distinguished themselves at the Battle of Palestro (31 May 1859, after which the Piedmontese monarch Victor Emmanuel II was appointed "honorary corporal" of the 3rd Regiment), at the Battle of Magenta (4 June 1859, during which they captured an Austrian flag) and at the Battle of Solferino (24 June 1859). In 1861 the Zouaves participated in the French expedition to Mexico that is commonly known as the "Mexican Adventure". Initially they provided just one battalion (the 2nd Battalion of the 2nd Regiment), but were later asked to send six *Bataillons de Marche* (the 1st Battalion and 2nd Battalion from each of the three regiments). To fight against the Mexican *guerrilleros* (insurgents) and to move more rapidly in the harsh terrain of Mexico, on 22 September 1864 one company of the 3rd Zouaves was mounted on mules and thus was temporarily transformed into a corps of mounted infantry. After the end of the unlucky Mexican Adventure the Zouaves were involved into the Franco-Prussian War, which was a disaster for Napoleon III's Imperial France. The three regiments serving in North Africa were asked to provide three *Bataillons de Marche* each (the three active battalions of each regiment), which were respectively attached to the 1st Army Corps, 3rd Army Corps and 4th Army Corps. Despite distinguishing themselves on several occasions, the Zouaves could do nothing to change the outcome of the conflict.

After the defeat of Napoleon III at the Battle of Sedan (31 August – 2 September 1870) the surviving Zouaves continued to fight against the Prussians in small "temporary" battalions, which served in various areas of France. Meanwhile, in North Africa other "temporary" battalions of Zouaves had to be recruited to face the massive Algerian insurgency of 1871. Following the end of both conflicts, the Zouaves were completely reorganized during 1872. With the disbandment of the Imperial Guard, the Zouaves who had been part of the latter were transformed into the new 4th Regiment of Zouaves. All the Zouave units were now to consist of four battalions with six companies each. On 10 January 1873 France's III Republic promulgated a new conscription law, according to which the Zouave regiments could also now consist of conscripts and no more only of volunteers. In 1875 the number of companies in each battalion was reduced to five (four active and one depot). In 1876 a second depot company was added to each battalion and each regiment was asked to send one of its depot companies to Arles, where a centralized depot of the Zouaves was established. On 9 February 1899 a 5th Battalion, stationed in France, was added to each regiment. During the period 1876–1914 the Zouaves participated in several colonial campaigns outside North Africa, such as Tonkin 1883–1885 (1st Battalion of the 1st Regiment and 1st Battalion of the 3rd Regiment), Annam 1887 (3rd Battalion of the 2nd Regiment) and China 1900–1901 (with a *Régiment de Marche* consisting of the 4th Battalion of the 2nd Regiment and of a provisional battalion created with companies of the 1st and 4th Regiment). On 23 December 1912, during the operations in Morocco, it was decided to create some additional battalions of Zouaves, one each for the 1st and 2nd Regiment, two for the 3rd Regiment and three for the 4th Regiment (thus bringing the total of active battalions to 23).

NCO of the Zouaves wearing M1836 uniform.

Private (left) and NCO (right) of the Zouaves wearing M1836 uniform.

Uniforms and weapons

The famous uniform of the French Zouaves was already defined in a quite precise way upon the corps' formation, on 1st October 1830. The new light infantrymen would be dressed in Moorish style (*habillement more*) with a quite exotic uniform that comprised the following elements: red cap (*calotte*) with green turban, dark blue long-sleeved vest (*à la turque*, i.e. in Turkish style), dark blue sleeveless *gilet* (waistcoat) and dark blue short trousers worn under loose *culottes* of the same colour. The companies made up of French soldiers wore their red caps without the green turban, which was a distinctive element of the companies recruited locally. On 15 December 1831, with the formation of the 2nd Zouave Battalion, a new version of the early uniform described above was introduced. The *culottes* became *garance* red and started to be decorated with dark blue embroidering on both sides. At the same time the *veste* received red trimming on the external edges and was decorated, on each side, with an S-shaped knot (known as *arabesque*) in red. The waist-sash, whose colour had not yet been regularized, became red for the 1st Battalion and light blue for the 2nd Battalion. In late 1832, after the fusion of the two existing battalions into a single unit, the latter adopted the uniform introduced for the former 2nd Battalion but with a red turban. With the progression of time, the waistcoat started to also have red trimming around the neck. Footwear, from 1830, consisted of black shoes that were worn with white spats (*guêtres*) and with yellow leather *jambières*. The latter could have black stripes on the external edges and under the side-buttons that closed them. On 6 July 1836 new dress regulations were promulgated for the Zouaves, but just a few modifications were introduced. The turban, which was now worn by all companies, became again green, a dark blue tassel was added on the back of the *calotte*, the red piping to the pointed cuffs of the vest was standardized, the trousers lost their previous decorative embroidering and the rear seam of the vest's forearms became opened to show a red lining and red thread loops engaging with brass ball buttons. This new uniform remained in use until 1852, when the number of Zouave regiments was increased from one to three. The NCOs' rank was shown by yellow inverted *chevrons* applied above the pointed cuffs, while the years of service of both rankers and NCOs were shown by red inverted *chevrons* applied on the left sleeve. Until 1842 the uniforms of Zouave officers were not regulated and thus the latter could wear the ordinary line infantry dress or the same dress of their men but with golden embroidery instead of the standard red. On 19 July 1842 a new model of tunic was introduced for the officers of the French light infantry and was soon also adopted by the Zouave ones. This was dark blue, without piping, and had nine ball buttons on the front. Rank was shown on it by golden *epaulettes*. The tunic was worn with the M1842 *casquette d'Afrique*, a peculiar headgear introduced for the troops serving in Africa that resembled a shako; this was red with dark blue bottom band and golden piping (showing rank) for officers. Initially the Zouaves were equipped with M1822 flintlock musket and with M1816 *sabre-briquette*. The latter was soon replaced with the M1831 *sabre-poignard*, while the former was substituted with the M1822t percussion musket in 1840. The Zouaves never received the new M1842 percussion musket as in 1852 they were issued with the rifled M1848 *carabine à tige* (stem carbine). Until 1837 the personal equipment of a Zouave consisted of a black leather waistbelt, a black leather ammunition pouch carried on the back of the waistbelt, a black leather bayonet scabbard carried on the right side and a black leather short sword scabbard carried on the left side. These elements were supplemented with locally-manufactured canteens and haversacks. In 1837 the ventral ammunition pouch, designed specifically for the Zouaves, came into use together with the M1828 infantry knapsack. On 13 February 1852, with the reorganization of the Zouaves into three regiments, a new uniform was introduced. This consisted of the following elements: dark blue *veste* with red trimming on the edges, red piping to the pointed cuffs and red S-shaped knot embroidered on each side, red lining and five brass ball buttons on the forearms, dark blue *sédria* waistcoat with red piping

NCO of the Zouaves wearing M1836 uniform.

around the neck and on the front, *garance* red loose trousers with dark blue decorative embroidery on the sides, light blue waist-sash, brown leather *jambières*, white spats and black shoes. The headgear continued to consist of a red *calotte* or *chéchia*, with dark blue tassel and green turban. On campaign, however, most of the Zouaves wore their *chéchia* without turban. The rank distinctions of senior NCOs remained yellow, while those of junior NCOs became *garance* red. Years of service continued to be shown by scarlet red inverted *chevrons*. The bottom loop of the vest's frontal knots, known as *tombò*, was in the distinctive colour of each regiment: red for the 1st, white for the 2nd and yellow for the 3rd. With the dress regulations of 1852 the officers of the Zouaves received a new tunic, of the same kind used by their equivalents of the light infantry, which was worn with *garance* trousers like the previous one. The new tunic was dark blue and did not have piping. It had three golden buttons on the forearms and golden *epaulettes* on the shoulders. This was worn together with the new visored *képi* introduced on 29 April 1852, which was red with dark blue bottom band and golden quarter-piping showing rank. The weaponry of the Zouaves did not change during the period 1852–1854, while the old personal equipment was replaced by a new design in 1853. The latter comprised white leather waistbelt, black leather ammunition pouch carried on the back of the waistbelt, black leather bayonet scabbard carried on the right side and black leather short sword scabbard carried on the left side. These elements were supplemented with the M1845 knapsack designed for the French light infantry and with a tin canteen. The uniform introduced in 1852 for the Zouaves remained unchanged until the end of Napoleon III's Second Empire and thus was used during the Crimean War, Second Italian War of Independence, Mexican Adventure and Franco-Prussian War. Once in Mexico, however, the *bataillons de marche* of Zouaves had to adapt their dress to the tropical climate of Central America. As a result, simple non-regulation attires became extremely popular. The headgear, waist-sash,

Zouaves fighting in Crimea; they are all wearing their headgear without turban. ASKB

jambières and spats remained those prescribed by the official dress regulations, but the vest and waistcoat, instead, were replaced by a loose white blouse made of cotton. This had no collar and bore red rank stripes on the sleeves. From 1853 the Zouaves received a pair of white trousers having the same cut as the ordinary *garance* ones, which were worn on most occasions especially during hot months. These, of course, were of general use in Mexico. In 1858 the Zouave regiments received the new M1853 light infantry carbine and the M1842 *sabre-baionette*, which they used until 1869 when they received the new M1866 Chassepot with bayonet. With the adoption of the new light infantry carbine, in 1858, the belt equipment also changed and a new scabbard for the *sabre-baionette* was introduced. In 1869 the Zouaves received the new ammunition pouches designed for use with the Chassepot and the new M1869 knapsack introduced for the French light infantry. Meanwhile, during the period 1852–1870, the Zouaves also replaced some components of their original personal equipment with new "standardized" ones: a *bidon* or canteen and a *gamelle* or mess tin were introduced in 1853, a new model of knapsack was introduced in 1854 and a *musette de toile* or haversack was introduced in 1862. The elite Zouaves of the Imperial Guard received an extremely elegant uniform soon after their formation, on 13 March 1855. This was quite similar to that adopted in 1852 by the existing Zouave regiments but had some peculiarities: the red *chéchia* had white turban and golden tassel, both the dark blue vest and waistcoat had golden trimming and embroidery, the pointed cuffs of the *veste* were red with golden piping, the side-decorations on the *garance* trousers were golden, the brass buckle of the waistbelt bore a flaming grenade and the black leather ammunition pouch bore a brass badge depicting an Imperial Eagle. Following the fall of Napo-

Zouave of the Crimean War, drinking from his canteen. ASKB

Zouave of the Crimean War. ASKB

leon III, the Zouaves of the Imperial Guard were transformed into the 4th Regiment of Zouaves and received the same uniform worn since 1852 by all the other Zouave units (with dark blue *tombò*). The officers of the Zouaves of the Imperial Guard were dressed like their equivalents of the other Zouave regiments, but with some distinctive features: the collar of their tunic bore a golden flaming grenade, their trousers had a broad golden side-stripe and they wore one golden *aiguillette* (decorative cord) on the right shoulder. In 1859 the Zouaves of the Imperial Guard received the new M1859 light infantry carbine, which was not distributed to the other Zouave units. In 1868 they were re-equipped with the M1866 Chassepot. Following the end of the Franco-Prussian War, the uniform of the Zouaves did not change in any significant way. In 1872 the turban became white for all the regiments, but started to be worn only on parade. On 28 January 1874 the leather *jambières* were replaced with the new dark blue *guêtres de campagne* (campaign spats). The new dress regulations promulgated for the whole French Army on 15 March 1879, which mostly remained valid until 1914, changed the Zouave's dress only in some details. White spats were introduced for parade use, the dark blue tassel started to be removed from the headgear on campaign, the white trousers (*pantalon de toile*) became standard issue for campaign use and the lining and brass buttons were removed from the vest's forearms. In 1889 the inverted *chevrons* showing years of service became *garance* red. In 1905 the Zouaves received the same dark blue puttees used by the French mountain infantry and thus started to wear their previous *guêtres de campagne* only on parade. During the colonial campaigns fought in Asia by the French in the period 1885–1900, the units of the Army of Africa replaced their standard headgear with the simple *casque colonial* that was made of cork. In 1883 the officers of the Zouaves replaced their previous tunics with a black *dolman* closely resembling a patrol jacket. This had black piping to the front, bottom edge, pointed cuffs and side-pockets. On the front it had a single vertical row with seven golden buttons and seven horizontal rows of black frogging. The *dolman* had black shoulder knots and silver Hungarian knots on the sleeves showing rank. The collar was red. The new jacket was worn with *garance* trousers (no longer in the traditional Zouave loose cut) having black side-stripe. In 1873 the Zouave officers received a new model of *képi*, red with dark blue bottom band and golden quarter-piping showing rank. In 1884 this was replaced by a new and smaller *képi*, which remained in use until 1914. In 1893 the *dolman* was replaced by a new model of tunic, black and single-breasted, having seven golden buttons on the front. This had black cuff flaps with three buttons each, golden rank rings around the cuffs, golden shoulder bars and red collar with black patches. In 1876 the Zouaves replaced their Chassepots with the M1874 Gras rifle, which remained in use until 1886. During the latter year they received the new M1886 Lebel rifle, which remained in use until 1914. During the period 1870–1914 the Zouaves changed several components of their personal equipment, adopting the following: M1879 and M1893 haversack; M1877, M1886 and M1892 ammunition pouches (all carried on the front of the waistbelt). On campaign non-regulation ammunition pouches worn across the chest on a crossbelt were quite popular.

Native officer of the Zouaves of the Imperial Guard. ASKB

Drum-major (left) and sapper (right) of the Zouaves of the Imperial Guard. Note the peculiar badge and equipment of the sapper.

Opposte page: Drum-major of the Zouaves of the Imperial Guard. ASKB

E. Grammont

Privates of the Zouaves of the Imperial Guard.

Trumpeter of the Zouaves of the Imperial Guard in campaign dress.

Zouaves of the Imperial Guard on campaign. ASKB

Zouaves of the Imperial Guard in their camp. ASKB

Zouaves of the 3rd Regiment (left) and of the 2nd Regiment (right) in 1876.

Zouave of the 2nd Regiment in parade dress, 1900.

Zouave of the 2nd Regiment in campaign dress, 1900.

Drum-major and musicians of the 3rd Zouave Regiment in campaign dress, 1900. ASKB

Zouave of the 4th Regiment in campaign dress, 1900. ASKB

NCO of the 3rd Zouave Regiment in 1914. ASKB

Privates (left) and NCO (right) of the Zouaves photographed at the beginning of the Great War.

The Tirailleurs

History and organization

Soon after their occupation of Algiers the French, in addition to the regular Zouaves, started to recruit some local units of native auxiliaries from the former soldiers of Algeria's Ottoman garrison. These continued to be commanded by their own officers and did not wear uniforms; as a result, they were an irregular corps. In February 1831 a first infantry company of Turks was organized in Oran from a few Janissaries who had decided to remain in Algeria, and in March 1832 a Turkish infantry battalion was formed in Bône. During 1833 a second company was raised in Oran, which was followed by an entire battalion during the early weeks of 1834. This new Turkish unit initially had three companies, which were later increased to five with the addition of the two independent companies that already existed in Oran.

Algerian auxiliary infantryman in French service, 1830.

In 1837 the Turkish Battalion of Oran, however, was disbanded due to its indiscipline and was replaced with a single infantry company that was made up of its most reliable elements. The Turkish Battalion of Bône, instead, performed quite well on several occasions and thus was retained in service by the French. On 17 November 1837 the unit recruited from the former Ottoman garrison of Bône was transformed into a half-battalion, but a new Turkish Battalion of Constantine was created with some of its best elements. The latter unit had French officers and NCOs, unlike the others that did not comprise French individuals. Initially no native units were raised from the province of Algiers, since the latter provided the native soldiers for the Zouaves. In 1839, however, four companies of *Tirailleurs* (light infantrymen) were raised from the surroundings of the Algerian capital. In January 1840 the French authorities decided to raise a full battalion, known as *Bataillon de Tirailleurs indigènes d'Algiers et du Titteri*, from the Turkish and Algerian individuals who wished to serve under their flag. This new corps consisted of six companies, while the Turkish Battalion of Constantine had nine companies. On 5 July 1840 another two light infantry companies were raised from the surroundings of Algiers and were united with the four ones organized in 1839 to form the new "Native Half-Battalion of Titteri" (the latter being a mountain region located not far from Algiers). The new corps of native infantry performed quite well on several occasions, showing the French that they had great military potential. As a result, in the autumn of 1841, it was decided that each of the three Algerian provinces (Algiers, Oran and Constantine) should have two battalions of native infantry. The Native Half-Battalion of Titteri was transformed into a battalion for the province of Algiers and two new units (the Turkish Battalion of Mostaganem and the Turkish Battalion of Oran) were raised in the province of Oran. All the new battalions had French superior officers and native junior ones.

On 7 December 1841 General Bugeaud, who much appreciated the combat capabilities of the Algerian natives, decided to transform the six existing battalions of irregular infantry into three battalions of regular infantry. The members of the latter would be known as Tirailleurs and would be dressed similarly to the Zouaves, who sent their remaining native elements to the new Tirailleur battalions. The *Bataillon de Tirailleurs indigènes d'Algiers et du Titteri* was merged with the Native Battalion of

Titteri to form the new 1st Tirailleur Battalion of Algiers (with six companies). The Turkish Battalion of Mostaganem and the Turkish Battalion of Oran were assembled together to form the new 2nd Tirailleur Battalion of Oran (with four companies), whilst the Turkish Battalion of Bône and the Turkish Battalion of Constantine were merged to form the new 3rd Tirailleur Battalion of Constantine (with eight companies). With the outbreak of the Crimean War, the Tirailleurs were called to serve overseas for the first time in their history. In the spring of 1854, in fact, each of the three battalions – which were now all structured on eight companies – was asked to provide six of its companies for the formation of a *Régiment de Marche de Tirailleurs Algériens*. The latter, consisting of two battalions with nine companies each, participated with distinction to several engagements: Alma (20 September 1854), Inkerman (5 November 1854) and Malakoff (7 September 1855). In Crimea they won their nickname of *Turcos* or "Turks", since the Russians – judging from their oriental-style uniforms – considered them as part of the Ottoman Army.

Meanwhile, on 9 January 1855, one new battalion of Tirailleurs had been raised from each Algerian province in order to replace the native soldiers who were fighting in Crimea. Before the conflict with Russia came to an end, on 18 October 1855, it was decided to unite the two battalions of each province to

Algerian auxiliary infantryman in French service, 1830.

Algerian auxiliary infantryman in French service, 1830.

form three regiments of Tirailleurs. Each of the latter would consist of three battalions with six companies. In 1859, due to France's participation in the Second Italian War of Independence, each of the three Tirailleur regiments was required to provide one of its battalions for the formation of a *Régiment de Marche* that was sent to Italy. This fought very well at Magenta and Solferino, having the honour to parade for the first time in its history in Paris following the end of the hostilities.

In 1860 each regiment of Tirailleurs was asked to provide two of its companies for the formation of a temporary *Bataillon de Marche* that was sent to Senegal. Here the Tirailleurs were taken as an example to follow for the new Battalion of Senegalese Tirailleurs that had been created just three years before. Another *Bataillon de Marche*, always with two companies provided by each of the three regiments, served in Cochinchina during 1861–1864. In present-day Vietnam the Tirailleurs played a major role in establishing an early form of French colonial presence but suffered greatly from tropical diseases.

In October 1862 a new *Bataillon de Marche* was organized with the usual structure of six companies and was sent to Mexico. Here the Tirailleurs were mostly tasked with escorting the convoys transporting supplies that moved from the port of Vera Cruz to Mexico City. In order to increase their mobility and to counter the rapid attacks of the local insurgents in a more effective way, the Tirailleurs were temporarily mounted on mules and thus acted as mounted infantry. On 17 November 1865, before the end of the Mexican Adventure, the number of battalions in each regiment of Tirailleurs was increased from three to four.

During the whole period 1863–1870 a single rotating battalion of Tirailleurs was always attached to the Zouaves of the Imperial Guard and thus served in France. Napoleon III, in fact, wanted to include in his guard at least one detachment of all the

Algerian Tirailleur with M1842 uniform.

various corps that made up the French Army. With the outbreak of the Franco-Prussian War, the three regiments of Tirailleurs were asked to send three of their four battalions to France. These were organized into three *Régiments de Marche* with three battalions each; these were attached to the following divisions of the 1st Army Corps: 1st Regiment to the 2nd Division, 2nd Regiment to the 3rd Division and 3rd Regiment to the 4th Division. The Tirailleurs, like most of the French Army, were wiped out at the Battle of Sedan. Thanks to the arrival of the new 4th Tirailleur Regiment that had been recently raised in Algeria, however, their survivors could be reorganized as a single *Régiment de Marche* that continued to fight until the end of the hostilities. After the Franco-Prussian War the Tirailleurs, on 3 February 1872, went back to their previous structure with three regiments. Each of the latter was now to consist of four battalions with six companies plus two companies of regimental depot (the latter were reduced to one in 1875). Since no form of conscription was introduced in 1873 for Algeria, the Tirailleurs continued to consist of volunteers.

On 12 May 1881 Tunisia became a French protectorate, following the signing of the Bardo Treaty. Initially the French decided to not disband the Tunisian Army and thus re-organized it as 12 independent "companies". These were "mixed" units of infantry, cavalry and artillery, with Tunisian rankers, Algerian NCOs and French officers. Each company comprised 200 infantrymen, 50 cavalrymen and 50 artillerymen. In December 1883, however, the French authorities decided to disband what remained of the Tunisian Army and used the native members of the independent companies to form the new *Garde Beylicale*, or Guard of the Beylik. Tunisia was not a colony of France but a protectorate, and as a result the local monarch, known as Beylik, was not forced to abdicate by the French and was permitted to have a small ceremonial guard. This consisted of 500 men and continued to exist until Tunisia became independent from France in 1956. It comprised one company of infantry with 200 soldiers, one company of cavalry with 100 soldiers and one company of artillery with 100 soldiers.

Algerian Tirailleur with M1842 uniform.

On 14 December 1884 the 4th Tirailleur Regiment, which had already existed during the Franco-Prussian War, was re-raised by recruiting Tunisians. The new unit, despite being numbered in sequence with the three Algerian regiments, was entirely made up of Tunisians. During 1885 a 5th and a 6th Battalion were added to each of the existing regiments. For the Tonkin War of 1883–1886 a "Provisional African Regiment" was formed to fight against the Chinese. This consisted of one battalion provided by the 1st Tirailleur Regiment, one battalion provided by the 3rd Tirailleur Regiment and one battalion provided by the Foreign Legion. This composite unit fought extremely well, but suffered heavy losses. In 1895, for the expedition to Madagascar, a "Provisional Algerian Regiment" was organized, consisting of one battalion provided by the Foreign Legion, one with two companies from the 1st Tirailleur Regiment and two companies from the 2nd Tirailleur Regiment, one with four companies from the 3rd Tirailleur Regiment. On 15 April 1913, after conscription was also introduced in the French territories of North Africa during 1912, five new regiments of Tirailleurs were raised. Only one of these, the 8th Regiment, was made up of Tunisians.

Uniforms and weapons

Until the organization of the regular Tirailleurs on 7 December 1841, the irregular foot auxiliaries supporting the French troops in Algeria did not have a proper uniform since they were dressed according to the personal tastes of their commanders. Most of the auxiliary infantry corps existing before 1842, however, were dressed in light blue quite similarly to the mounted

Native officer of the Algerian Tirailleurs with M1853 uniform. ASKB

Gendarmes Maures. In 1842 the Tirailleur Battalion of Algiers was the first to receive the new uniform prescribed during December of the previous year, which was very similar to the exotic *habillement more* used by the Zouaves. This consisted of the following elements: red *chéchia* or *calotte* with light blue tassel and white turban having light blue vertical stripes, medium green long-sleeved vest (*à la turque*, i.e. in Turkish style), *garance* red sleeveless *gilet* (waistcoat) and *garance* red loose *culottes* decorated with yellow embroidering on both sides. The *veste* had yellow trimming around the neck and on the external edges and was decorated, on each side, with an S-shaped knot in yellow. The pointed cuffs of the vest were piped in yellow and the rear seam of its forearms was opened to show a yellow lining and yellow thread loops engaging with brass ball buttons. Footwear consisted of black shoes that were worn with white spats (*guêtres*) and with yellow leather *jambières*. The latter had black stripes on the external edges and under the side-buttons that closed them. A scarlet red waist-sash completed the outfit. On 12 April 1843 this uniform was officially issued to all the regular battalions of Tirailleurs. Its adoption, however, encountered a strong resistance since most of the Algerian infantrymen did not like the green colour of the new *veste* (which was the same of the French dragoons' uniform) and thus preferred to continue wearing their old light blue dress. By 1845, however, all battalions were dressed in green. From 1849 the *chéchia* started to be worn without turban. The NCOs' rank was shown by yellow inverted *chevrons* applied above the pointed cuffs, while the years of service of both rankers and NCOs were shown by red inverted *chevrons* applied on the left sleeve.

In 1842 the French officers of the Tirailleurs adopted the new model of tunic that was introduced for the officers of the French light infantry on 19 July of that year. This was medium green, without piping, and had nine ball buttons on the front. Rank was shown by golden *epaulettes*. The tunic was worn with the M1842 *casquette d'Afrique*, which was red with green bottom band and golden piping (showing rank) for officers. Native officers, instead, were uniformed like the rankers but had the trimming and embroidery of both their vests and waistcoats in gold. Their rank was shown by golden inverted *chevrons* applied above the pointed cuffs. Initially the Tirailleurs were equipped with M1822t percussion musket and with the M1831 *sabre-poignard*. During this whole period the Tirailleurs had the same personal equipment used by the Zouaves.

On 14 February 1853 the Tirailleurs, following their re-

Private (left) and NCO (right) of the Algerian Tirailleurs fighting in Crimea.

organization in three regiments, received a new light blue uniform that would remain in use until 1914 with very little modification. This, like the previous one, was quite similar to the dress worn by the Zouaves but had the same colours of the uniforms used by the irregular Algerian foot troops before 1842. It consisted of the following elements: light blue *veste* with yellow trimming on the edges, yellow piping to the pointed cuffs and yellow S-shaped knot embroidered on each side, yellow lining and five brass ball buttons on the forearms, light blue *sédria* waistcoat with yellow piping around the neck and on the front, light blue loose trousers with yellow decorative embroiderings on the sides, red waist-sash, brown leather *jambières*, white spats and black shoes. The bottom loop of the vest's frontal knots, known as *tombò*, was in the distinctive colour of each regiment: *garance* red for the 1st Regiment, white for the 2nd Regiment and *jonquille* yellow for the 3rd Regiment. The rank distinctions of NCOs remained yellow, while the years of service continued to be shown by scarlet red inverted *chevrons*. The headgear was now to consist of a red *calotte* or *chéchia*, with light blue tassel and white turban.

With the dress regulations of 1853 the French officers of the Tirailleurs received a new tunic, of the same kind used by their equivalents of the light infantry, which was worn with *garance* trousers like the previous one. The new tunic was light blue and did not have piping, it had three golden buttons on the forearms and golden *epaulettes* on the shoulders. This was worn together with the new visored *képi* introduced on 29 April 1852, which was red with light blue bottom band and golden quarter-piping showing rank. The native officers of the Tirailleurs were dressed like their men, but with trimming and embroidery of both their vest and waistcoat in gold. Their decorative embroidery were much larger and more complex than those worn by NCOs/rankers. Their rank was shown by golden Hungarian knots embroidered on the sleeves. With the reorganization of 1853 the Tirailleurs adopted the M1842 infantry musket, which they continued to use until 1857 when they received the new M1853 one (modified in order to be rifled).

The uniform introduced in 1853 for the Tirailleurs remained unchanged until the end of Napoleon III's Second Empire and thus was used during the Crimean War, Mexican Adventure and Franco-Prussian War. Once in Mexico, however, the Tirailleurs had to adapt themselves to the local combat environment. Like the Zouaves, on several occasions they were employed as mounted infantrymen in order to counter

Privates (left) and NCO (right) of the 1st Regiment of Algerian Tirailleurs in 1860. ASKB

the bands of insurgents (*guerrilleros*) operating in the Mexican countryside. As a result, the Algerian light infantrymen were mounted on mules and were given cavalry sabres. According to contemporary sources they performed extremely well as counter-guerrilla soldiers, despite having never been trained to move on mules. The *Turcos* were particularly feared by the Mexicans, who considered them as the best fighters of the French military forces. The Tirailleurs received the M1866 Chassepot rifle only after the end of the Mexican Adventure, in 1868. From 1853 the Tirailleurs received a pair of white trousers having the same cut as the ordinary light blue ones, which were worn on most occasions especially during hot months; these, of course, were of general use in Tonkin. The white *casque colonial* made of cork was worn during several colonial campaigns of the late 19th century (Madagascar, Tonkin, Dahomey).

Following the end of the Franco-Prussian War, the uniform of the Tirailleurs did not change in any significant way. From 1872 the turban started to be worn only on parade and in 1874 the leather *jambières* were replaced with the new dark blue *guêtres de campagne* (campaign spats). The new dress regulations promulgated for the whole French Army on 15 March 1879 changed the Tirailleur's dress only in some details. White spats were introduced for parade use, the light blue tassel started to be removed from the headgear on campaign and the white trousers (*pantalon de toile*) became standard issue for campaign use. The lining and brass buttons were removed from the vest's forearms. When the Regiment of Tunisian Tirailleurs was created in 1884 it adopted the same uniform as the Algerian Tirailleurs, with light blue *tombò*. In 1889 the inverted *chevrons* showing years of service became *garance* red and in 1905 the Tirailleurs received the same dark blue puttees used by the French mountain infantry and thus started to wear their previous *guêtres de campagne* only on parade. In 1883 the French officers of the Tirailleurs replaced their previous tunics with a light blue-grey *dolman* closely resembling a patrol jacket. This had black piping to the front, bottom edge, pointed cuffs and side-pockets. On the front it had a single vertical row with seven golden buttons and seven horizontal rows of black frogging. The *dolman* had black shoulder knots and silver Hungarian knots on the sleeves showing rank. The collar was yellow. The new jacket was worn with *garance* trousers with a light blue side-stripe. In 1873 the French officers of the Tirailleurs had received a new model of *képi*, red with light blue bottom band and golden quarter-piping showing rank. In 1884 this was replaced by a new and smaller *képi*, which remained in use until 1914. The uniform of native officers remained the same, but its colour was modified to become light blue-grey like that of the of the French officers' *dolman*. In addition, the trimming and embroidery of both its vest and waistcoat became black. In 1893 the French officers of the Tirailleurs replaced their *dolman* with a new model of tunic, light blue-grey and single-breasted, having seven golden buttons on the front. This had yellow cuff flaps with three buttons each, golden rank rings around the cuffs, golden shoulder bars and yellow collar with light blue patches. In 1876 the Tirailleurs replaced their Chassepots with the M1874 Gras rifle, which remained in use until 1886, when they received the new M1886 Lebel rifle, which remained in use until 1914.

Native officer (left) and NCO (right) of the 1st Regiment of Algerian Tirailleurs in 1868.

NCO of the 2nd Regiment of Algerian Tirailleurs with the guidon of his company. Note the presence of the "Hand of Allah" Muslim symbol on the guidon.

Native privates and French NCO of the Algerian Tirailleurs photographed during the Franco-Prussian War. ASKB

Native NCO (left) and private (right) of the Algerian Tirailleurs photographed during the Franco-Prussian War. ASKB

Native officer of the 4th Regiment of Tunisian Tirailleurs. On the back he has the wide-brimmed *tarazala* straw hat, which was extremely popular in southern Algeria and Tunisia.

Private of the 1st Regiment of Algerian Tirailleurs in campaign dress, 1900. The headgear is worn without turban.

Native NCO of the 1st Regiment of Algerian Tirailleurs in campaign dress, 1900. ASKB

French officer and soldiers of the 2nd Regiment of Algerian Tirailleurs, 1910. ASKB

Private of the Algerian Tirailleurs photographed in France at the beginning of the Great War.

The Chasseurs d'Afrique

History and organization

The French expeditionary corps that captured Algiers in 1830 comprised a temporary regiment of Mounted Chasseurs (light cavalry), consisting of three squadrons. Two of the latter were taken from the 17th Regiment of Mounted Chasseurs (one of which was equipped with lances) and one was taken from the 13th Regiment of Mounted Chasseurs. After the defeat of the Ottoman military forces, the single squadron of the 13th Regiment was soon sent back to France. The other two squadrons, instead, came back to Europe only during the last weeks of 1831. In order to patrol the surroundings of Algiers in a proper way and to have a sufficient number of horsemen at their disposal, the French soon started to plan the raising of some local cavalry units made up of Algerian natives. On 9 October 1830 the French authorities decided to organize three squadrons of "Mounted Zouaves", recruited from the Zwawa communities living around Algiers. The Kabyle Zwawa tribes had provided excellent cavalry contingents to the Ottomans for a long time and thus the French were interested in employing them as mounted auxiliaries. The three new squadrons (later reduced to two) soon became known as *Chasseurs Algériens* and adopted an early version of the future Spahis' uniform. Their members had a distinctive irregular nature and were armed with infantry muskets, since they were to operate more like a sort of mounted gendarmerie than as true cavalry. Following the success of the *Chasseurs Algériens*, the French recruited another two units of native cavalry, one squadron of *Chasseurs Numides* and one squadron of *Guides*. When the two remaining squadrons of metropolitan Mounted Chasseurs were sent back to France, however, it became clear that a new cavalry corps having a more "regular" nature had to be formed in Algeria. As a result, on 17 November 1831, the *Chasseurs Algériens* were disbanded and their members were united with those troopers of the 17th Mounted Chasseurs Regiment who volunteered to remain in Africa in order to create a new corps. This, formed on 17 November 1831, assumed the denomination of *Chasseurs d'Afrique* or African Chasseurs. Like

Officer of the African Chasseurs with M1831 uniform.

the early Zouaves it was going to be a *corps mixte* comprising local recruits but also French volunteers. The new corps would be made up of two cavalry regiments, one stationed in Algiers and one stationed in Oran. Like the early Zouaves, the African Chasseurs did not become famous for their discipline and mutinied on two occasions during the first years of their life.

The 1st Regiment of African Chasseurs was formed quite easily, since it absorbed the two squadrons of Algerian Chasseurs. Originally it was to have just four squadrons, but these were augmented to eight by the end of 1832. The 2nd Regiment of African Chasseurs was organized more slowly, but it finally came to have six squadrons instead of the four ones originally planned. In December 1832 the French decided to raise a 3rd Regiment of African Chasseurs by assembling together the last two squadrons of the 1st Regiment with two squadrons of irregular cavalrymen (which had been recruited during the previous months). On 27 July 1834 the French authorities organized the first regular corps of native cavalrymen, known as *Spahis Réguliers d'Algiers*. As a result, the Algerian elements of the 1st Regiment of African Chasseurs (the former *Chasseurs Algériens*) were detached from their parent unit in order to form the new corps. Following this organizational change, the 1st Regiment of African Chasseurs started to have five squadrons instead of the previous six. Over time the presence of Algerian elements inside the *Chasseurs d'Afrique* became increasingly less significant. The native soldiers of the 1st Regiment became the *Spahis Réguliers d'Algiers*, the 2nd Regiment had just one squadron made up of Algerian elements and the 3rd Regiment consisted almost entirely of French volunteers. On 23 December 1839 the 6th Squadron of the 2nd Regiment and the 6th Squadron of the 3rd Regiment were assembled together in order to form the new 4th Regiment of African Chasseurs. As a result, by the beginning of 1840, each of the four units of *Chasseurs d'Afrique* had five squadrons and the native soldiers now made up two squadrons in the 1st Regiment, two squadrons in the 2nd Regiment, one squadron in the 3rd Regiment and one squadron in the 4th Regiment.

On 7 December 1841, with the creation of the Spahis and with the complete reorganization of the native cavalry corps, the *Chasseurs d'Afrique* ceased to be a *corps mixte* and started to be made up only of French volunteers. The four regiments of African Chasseurs replaced their native elements – who became part of the Spahis – with new French recruits and thus retained their previous structure with six squadrons. With the reorganization of 1841–1842 the *Chasseurs d'Afrique* lost their original "mounted infantry" character and became proper light cavalrymen. Each of the four regiments was stationed in a major Algerian city, the 1st at Algiers, the 2nd at Oran, the 3rd at Constantine and the 4th at Bône. When the Crimean War broke out, the African Chasseurs had already won a solid reputation as harsh fighters. During the period 1842–1845, in fact, they took part in all the major engagements fought by the French against the insurgents of Abd al-Qādir. With the beginning of the new conflict, the four regiments of *Chasseurs d'Afrique* were asked to provide four squadrons each for the operations against the Russians. Each of them also formed a 7th and 8th Squadron, which were to remain in North Africa for the duration of the hostilities and which were to act as depot units. The 16 squadrons sent to the Ottoman Empire

Officers of the African Chasseurs with M1831 uniform.

were assembled into two temporary brigades: the 1st Brigade, consisting of the squadrons provided by the 1st and 4th Regiment, commanded by General d'Allonville; the 2nd Brigade, consisting of the squadrons provided by the 2nd and 3rd Regiment, was commanded by General de Cassaignoles. Like the Zouaves, the African Chasseurs fought with great determination in Crimea. In particular, they participated in the Battle of Balaklava during which their 1st Brigade covered the retreat of what remained of the famous British Light Brigade. On 5 April 1856 the 4th Regiment of African Chasseurs was disbanded and its members, together with other elite soldiers coming from the French light cavalry, were employed to create the new Mounted Chasseur Regiment of the recently-formed Imperial Guard. Initially Napoleon III wanted to have a regiment of *Chasseurs d'Afrique* inside his guard, but in the end the new unit that was formed had the same standard character of the metropolitan Mounted Chasseurs. Following their return to Algeria, the remaining three regiments disbanded their depot squadrons and went back to their previous structure with six active squadrons.

The three regiments of African Chasseurs participated in the Second Italian War of Independence of 1859 with their full establishment, being part of the Cavalry Division commanded by General Desvaux. They distinguished themselves at the Battle of Solferino (24 June 1859), during which they suffered heavy losses. In 1860 the *Chasseurs d'Afrique* participated in the French expedition to China with a single squadron of the 2nd Regiment. During that same year another two squadrons (the 1st of the 1st Regiment and the 1st of the 3rd Regiment) took part in the French expedition to Lebanon. The latter was caused by the massacres of local Christians organized by the Muslims and saw the participation of a composite cavalry regiment that also included the two squadrons of African Chasseurs. The *Chasseurs d'Afrique* initially participated in the Mexican Adventure with just a small detachment of 25 men, but when the French involvement in Central America became larger each of their regiments was asked to send two squadrons. The six squadrons of African Chasseurs operating in Mexico were part of the Cavalry Brigade commanded by General de Mirandol. The squadrons provided by the 1st and 2nd Regiment were assembled together in order to form a 1st *Régiment de Marche de Cavalerie*, while the squadrons provided by the 3rd Regiment were assembled with those sent by the metropolitan 12th Regiment of Mounted Chasseurs to form a 2nd *Régiment de Marche de Cavalerie*. The African Chasseurs fought extremely well in Mexico and were particularly effective in conducting counter-guerrilla operations. As a result of their good performance, on 1st April 1867 Napoleon III decided to re-raise the 4th Regiment of African Chasseurs from depot detachments of the three existing units as well as of two metropolitan light cavalry regiments. With the outbreak of the Franco-Prussian War in 1870, the four regiments of *Chasseurs d'Afrique* were called to serve in France. They formed an independent Division of African Chasseurs commanded by General du Barail and consisting of two brigades. The 1st Brigade comprised the 1st and 3rd Regiment, the 2nd Brigade comprised the 2nd and 4th Regiment.

The *Chasseurs d'Afrique* serving in France during 1870–1871 suffered severe losses. Meanwhile, in North Africa, two provisional regiments with two squadrons each had to be created from the single depot squadron left in Algeria by each of the original regiments, in order to counter the actions of the Algerian insurgents. Following the end of the Franco-Prussian War the four regiments of *Chasseurs d'Afrique* were rapidly rebuilt, thanks in part to the promulgation of the new conscrip-

Trooper of the African Chasseurs (left) and trooper of the Gendarmes Maures (right) in the early 1830s. ASKB

tion law, according to which also the African Chasseurs could consist of conscripts. The internal structure with six squadrons was not modified. On 25 July 1887 the 6th Squadron of each regiment was detached from its parent unit and employed to form two new regiments of *Chasseurs d'Afrique* (the 5th and the 6th). During the period 1883–1914 detachments of the African Chasseurs were sent to serve overseas on several occasions. The 6th Squadron of the 1st Regiment was in the Far East during 1884–1886, in 1895 a single composite squadron – made up of platoons provided by all the regiments – fought in Madagascar and in 1900–1901 two small detachments from the 5th Regiment and 6th Regiment were sent to China. At the outbreak of World War I the *Chasseurs d'Afrique* consisted of six regiments with six squadrons each (five active and one depot).

Uniforms and weapons

The first uniform used by the African Chasseurs upon their formation on 17 November 1831 had a distinctive Polish character. It consisted of the following elements: black leather *czapka* with light blue central band and red squared upper part piped in light blue, having tricolour national cockade and decorative brass chain as well as black falling plume on the left side; light blue single-breasted tunic with pleated long skirt, yellow collar piped in light blue, brass *contre-epaulettes*, white metal buttons on the front and red decorative cords-and-flounders on the left side of the chest (attached also to the headgear); waist-sash with light blue and red horizontal stripes; red trousers with light blue side-stripe; white gloves and black leather boots. The shabraque was red with light blue external edging. The officers had golden *epaulettes* on the shoulders, while the trumpeters had the following uniform: black leather *czapka* with red central band and white squared upper part piped in red, having tricolour national cockade and decorative brass chain as well as white falling plume on the left side; red single-breasted tunic with pleated long skirt, yellow collar piped in white-and-red, brass *contre-epaulettes*, white metal buttons on the front and red-and-white decorative cords-and-flounders on the left side of the chest; waist-sash with light blue and red horizontal stripes; light blue trousers with red side-stripe; white gloves and black leather boots. Their shabraque was green with white external edging. The choice of the *czapka* as the headgear of the new African Chasseurs was not a casual one. The French authorities, in fact, knew that this Polish cap was a symbol of France's Napoleonic era and thus hoped that the possibility of wearing it could attract many young volunteers who wished to renew the glory of their country. Initially the *Chasseurs d'Afrique* were armed with the M1777 flintlock infantry musket, with the *An XIII* sabre for light cavalry, since they were to act as a sort of "mounted infantry". In 1833, however, it was decided to equip one half of the squadrons in each regiment of African Chasseurs with lances and the other half with M1816 artillery musketoons. The lances had a tricolour pennon in the national colours of France. They were

Officer (left) and trooper (right) of the two squadrons of *Chasseurs Algeriens*; the latter were part of the 1st Regiment of African Chasseurs. ASKB

phased out in 1838, when all the squadrons of *Chasseurs d'Afrique* started to be equipped with *An XIII* sabres and M1822 artillery musketoons. On 30 April 1839 the existing four regiments of African Chasseurs received a new uniform, much simpler than the previous one, that consisted of the following elements: red M1833 *casquette d'Afrique* with light blue bottom band and quarter piping, tricolour national cockade with light blue lace holder, brass regimental number and pompom in the distinctive colour of each regiment (light blue for the 1st, red for the 2nd, green for the 3rd and yellow for the 4th); light blue single-breasted tunic with pleated long skirt, yellow collar piped in light blue, brass *contre-epaulettes*, white metal buttons on the front and red decorative cords-and-flounders on the left side of the chest; waist-sash with light blue and red horizontal stripes; loose red trousers with light blue side-stripe ending in black "false boots"; white gloves. The shabraque and the white belt equipment did not change and officers continued to have golden *epaulettes*, while trumpeters simply had some distinctive white-and-red piping around the collar of their tunic. Like the previous uniform the NCOs' rank was shown by white inverted *chevrons* applied above the pointed cuffs (the latter had yellow piping), while the years of service of both rankers and NCOs were shown by red inverted *chevrons* applied on the left sleeve. In 1839, however, the African Chasseurs also received a practical campaign dress. This, instead of the long-skirted tunic, comprised a short light blue jacket that was worn tucked inside the trousers. The jacket had light blue collar with yellow patches and simple light blue shoulder straps; it had yellow piping to the pointed cuffs and was worn together with an entirely red waist-sash. In 1842 the old M1833 *casquette d'Afrique* was replaced with the new M1842 one, which had the same colours as its predecessor but a different shape. This remained in use until 1847, when it was replaced by a new and smaller version of the *casquette d'Afrique*. By the time of the Crimean War the *Chasseurs d'Afrique* had already been equipped for several years with the M1822t dragoon musket and had replaced it with the new M1842 one. The new sabre was the M1822 for light cavalry. The campaign short jacket introduced in 1839 remained in use, practically with no modifications, until 1873. As a result, it was also worn in Mexico where most of the *Chasseurs d'Afrique* added white covers to their headgear in order to have some protection from the tropical sun. The M1847 *casquette d'Afrique* continued to be worn by the African Chasseurs until 1873. This had a pompom in the distinctive colour of each regiment. It should be noted, however, that from 20 November 1858 they were also permitted to wear – with the campaign uniform – an alternative headgear. This was the Algerian *chéchia*, a red soft cap decorated with red tassel and three horizontal black stripes around its base. The weapons used in Mexico were M1822 light cavalry sabre and M1860 dragoon musket. In 1862 the *Chasseurs d'Afrique* replaced their parade uniform, introduced during 1839, with a new one. This was worn with the M1862 *casquette d'Afrique* (a slightly modified version of this headgear's previous model) and consisted of the following elements: light blue *dolman* with black piping to the front, bottom edge, yellow pointed cuffs and yellow collar; on the front this had a single

Trooper of the African Chasseurs with M1831 uniform. ASKB

vertical row with six white metal buttons and six horizontal rows of black frogging; *garance* red loose trousers with light blue double side-stripes ending with false boots for NCOs/troopers and being worn with black leather boots for officers. The NCOs' rank was now shown by yellow inverted *chevrons* applied above the pointed cuffs, while the years of service of both rankers and NCOs were shown by red inverted *chevrons* applied on the left sleeve. The officers' *dolman* had additional black embroidery between the rows of frogging and was worn together with a red waist-sash. Officers did not have false boots but standard black ones. In addition, they had silver Hungarian knots on the sleeves showing rank and wore the M1852 *képi* (red, with light blue bottom band and golden quarter-piping showing rank) as headgear. In 1867 a modified version of the officers' *képi*, known as M1867, was introduced. In 1866 the *Chasseurs d'Afrique* were re-equipped with M1866 cavalry carbines but continued to use M1822 light cavalry sabres.

In 1873 the *Chasseurs d'Afrique* adopted a new parade uniform, consisting of the following elements: light blue *dolman* with black piping to the front, bottom edge, light blue pointed cuffs and yellow collar. On the front this had three vertical rows with nine white metal buttons and nine horizontal rows of black frogging. The new *dolman* also had black shoulder knots. The NCOs' rank was now shown by scarlet red inverted *chevrons* applied above the pointed cuffs, while the years of service of both rankers and NCOs were shown by *garance* red inverted *chevrons* applied on the left sleeve. The officers' *dolman* had silver Hungarian knots on the sleeves showing rank. All ranks wore red trousers with light blue double side-stripes. With the parade dress both officers and rankers wore the new M1873 *casquette d'Afrique*, which closely resembled a standard *képi*. This was red with light blue bottom band and pompom in the distinctive colour of each regiment. It had golden quarter-piping showing rank for officers. In 1873 the African Chasseurs also received a new campaign dress, which remained in use with very little modifications – like the M1873 parade uniform – until 1914. On campaign the M1873 *casquette d'Afrique* was used with a white cover (khaki from 1913), while the *dolman* was replaced with a much simpler short jacket having a single row of white metal buttons on the front. The campaign jacket had shoulder knots made of white wool, yellow collar with light blue patches bearing the regimental number embroidered in yellow and yellow piping to the pointed cuffs. It was worn together with a red waist-sash and with red trousers having narrow single side-stripe. Rank distinctions were the same worn on the parade *dolman*. The officers used a slightly simplified version of their parade dress for campaign use. In 1899, however, they adopted the same M1892 single-breasted short tunic that had been introduced for the French light cavalry (retaining their distinctive light blue colour). This had a single row of seven buttons on the front and a standing collar. Being quite simple, it was worn for parade but also on campaign. In 1874 the African Chasseurs received the M1874 Gras cavalry carbine, which was replaced by the M1890 Lebel cavalry carbine in 1891. The M1822 light cavalry sabre remained in service until 1914, being used with a khaki cover from 1913.

Trumpeter of the African Chasseurs with M1831 uniform. ASKB

Sapper of the African Chasseurs with M1831 uniform. Note the peculiar badge and equipment. ASKB

African Chasseurs wearing M1839 campaign dress; the figure on the left has the M1833 *casquette d'Afrique*, while the figure on the right has a non-regulation visored cap. ASKB

Standard-bearer and NCOs of the 1st Regiment of African Chasseurs wearing M1839 parade dress. ASKB

Above, left: NCOs of the African Chasseurs (left), Zouaves (centre) and African Light Infantry (right) in 1840.

Above: NCO of the 1st Regiment of African Chasseurs with M1839 parade dress.

Trooper of the 1st Regiment of African Chasseurs fighting in Crimea.

Officer of the African Chasseurs wearing M1862 dress. ASKB

Opposite page: Trooper of the African Chasseurs wearing campaign uniform in 1860.

Trooper of the African Chasseurs with campaign uniform in the early 1860s.

Trooper of the 4th Regiment of African Chasseurs with M1862 dress.

Trooper of the 3rd Regiment of African Chasseurs with the campaign dress used in Mexico. Note the white cover of the headgear.

NCO of the 4th Regiment of African Chasseurs wearing campaign uniform in 1890.

Trooper of the 3rd Regiment of African Chasseurs with M1873 parade dress.

Trooper of the 3rd Regiment of African Chasseurs with M1873 campaign dress.

NCO of the African Chasseurs in campaign uniform, photographed at the beginning of the Great War.

The Spahis

History and organization

Before the arrival of the French, the Ottoman garrison of Algeria comprised a certain number of professional cavalrymen who were known as *Sipahi*; the latter term, transformed into "Spahis" by the French, continued to be used also after the French conquest of Algiers to indicate locally-recruited native horsemen. General Bourmont, before leaving North Africa after the July Revolution, decided to include two squadrons of native *Sipahi* inside the French military forces garrisoning Algiers; his successor, General Clauzel, confirmed this decision and thus three squadrons of *Chasseurs Algériens* (later reduced to two) were created. As we have already seen, these were soon absorbed into the newly-formed *Chasseurs d'Afrique* since the latter were – at least initially – a *corps mixte*. The former *Sipahi*, however, were not particularly enthusiast about the idea of serving in the African Chasseurs since they were not used to strict military discipline and wanted to be commanded by their own officers. As a result, on 10 September 1834, the French authorities raised a new native cavalry corps known as *Spahis réguliers d'Algiers*. This consisted of four squadrons with 200 men each and absorbed the former members of the *Chasseurs Algériens* who had been included into the 1st Regiment of African Chasseurs. On 12 August 1836 the *Spahis réguliers d'Algiers* were expanded from four to six squadrons; meanwhile, similar corps of regular native cavalrymen were also formed in Bône (on 10 June 1835) and in Oran (on 12 August 1836). These had four squadrons each and soon proved to be made up of reliable soldiers like the unit organized in Algiers. During this early period the French recruited also some irregu-

Native soldiers of the Gendarmes Maures (left), Algerian Spahis (centre) and Algerian Tirailleurs (right) in the early 1840s.

lar contingents of native horsemen: a single cavalry squadron made up of Turkish soldiers in Bône and a mixed unit (800 infantrymen and 200 cavalrymen) in Constantine. In September 1840 several new irregular corps of native cavalry were formed, one at Algiers, one at Sétif and three in the province of Constantine. Meanwhile the French had also organized a native gendarmerie, made up of horsemen and tasked with patrolling the countryside of Algiers. This, created in 1836, assumed the denomination of *Gendarmes Maures* or Moorish Gendarmes. It was originally structured on independent platoons attached to the French units of Gendarmerie, but on 5 July 1840 the corps was reorganized as follows: two squadrons in the province of Algiers (one patrolling the city and one patrolling the countryside), one platoon in Constantine, one platoon in Bône and one platoon in Philippeville. The officers of the *Gendarmes Maures* were all French and the unit performed quite well as an auxiliary police force.

On 7 December 1841, having understood that the Spahis had great military potential, the French decided to put order into the organization of their locally-recruited native cavalry. The Moorish Gendarmes and the units of irregular Spahis were all disbanded, in order to form a single and unified corps of regular Spahis. The latter was to consist of 20 independent squadrons, each of which had the following internal establishment: four French superior officers, three Algerian junior officers, 20 French NCOs and 173 Algerian junior NCOs or troopers. Overall command of the Spahis was given to the famous General Yusuf, a Corsican – originally named Joseph Vantini – who had spent most of his life in Tunisia and who had joined the French military forces during their early conquest of Algeria. Yusuf was a Muslim, had a great knowledge of the native traditions and spoke several local languages. As a result, he was particularly loved by his men and was extremely valuable to the French. The 20 squadrons of Spahis were distributed in the territory as follows: five in the province of Algiers, nine in the province of Constantine and ten in the province of Oran. On 21 July 1845 the organization based on independent squadrons was abandoned and the various units

Native officer (left) and trooper (right) of the Spahis réguliers d'Algiers. ASKB

French officer of the Algerian Spahis with M1841 "native" uniform.

Native trooper of the Algerian Spahis with M1841 uniform.

were assembled together in order to form three regiments: the 1st Spahis Regiment of Algiers, the 2nd Spahis Regiment of Oran and the 3rd Spahis Regiment of Constantine. Each of the latter was to consist of six squadrons, and one squadron of the 1st Regiment was detached from its parent unit and sent to Senegal, where it provided the cadres for the formation of the new Squadron of Senegalese Spahis.

At the outbreak of the Crimean War the Spahis were asked to form a single *Escadron de Marche* or temporary squadron, which was made up of volunteers coming from the three existing regiments. This unit did not see much combat against the Russians, since it acted as the mounted escort of the French expeditionary force's commander-in-chief. On 24 June 1854 the French authorities decided to raise a new unit of native cavalry, known as *Spahis d'Orient*, from the many *Bashi-Bazouks* or irregular fighters who were available in the Ottoman Empire. General Yusuf was ordered to form a semi-regular military corps from these undisciplined soldiers of fortune. The original plan was to form eight regiments of *Spahis d'Orient* with four squadrons each, but in the end not a single squadron became operational and thus the whole project was cancelled in August 1854 (after most of the *Bashi-Bazouks* deserted with the modern weapons that they had just received from the French). In 1860 a single squadron of the 2nd Spahis was sent to Lebanon and another squadron from the same regiment was sent to China, together with a squadron of the 2nd African Chasseurs. During the whole period 1863–1870 a single squadron of Spahis was always attached to the Mounted Chasseurs of the Imperial Guard and thus served in France. Napoleon III, in fact, wanted to include in his guard at least one detachment of all the various corps that made up the French Army. This squadron was made up of 150 men, since each of the three existing regiments of Spahis was asked to provide 50 of its best elements for the formation of this "special" unit. The Spahis did not participate to the Mexican Adventure, but some of their French officers and NCOs were sent to Central America where they provided some of the cadres for the new units of *Contre-Guérillas* (special units of the Gendarmerie, tasked with fighting against the Mexican insurgents and dressed with red *dolman* like the officers of the Spahis).

With the outbreak of the Franco-Prussian War the Spahis were asked to form a single *Escadron de Marche*, which was made up of 150 men (each of the existing three regiments provided 50 of the latter). This single unit of Spahis was attached to the Cousin Cavalry Brigade, which consisted of the metropolitan 1st and 9th Regiment of Mounted Chasseurs. On 19 October 1870, due to the military emergency caused by the Prussian victories, each regiment of Spahis was ordered to send 100 volunteers to France; these acted as cadres for the formation of a new corps known as *Éclaireurs Algériens*, which consisted of three squadrons with 300 men each (100 Spahis and 200 volunteers). Each of these squadrons comprised volunteers coming from one of the three Algerian provinces.

On 1st October 1886 the 4th Spahis Regiment, recruited from Tunisians, was organized. The new unit, despite being numbered in sequence with the three Algerian regiments, was entirely made up of Tunisians. On 6 June 1914, just a few weeks before the outbreak of World War I, the 6th Spahis Regiment (made up of Algerian soldiers) was created. During the period 1885–1914 the Spahis participated in some campaigns fought by the French Army overseas: the 3rd Squadron of the 1st Spahis, the 5th Squadron of the 2nd Spahis and the 1st Squadron of the 3rd Spahis were sent to Tonkin in 1885–1886; a few volunteers of the 3rd Spahis, instead, were attached to the single composite squadron of *Chasseurs d'Afrique* sent to Madagascar in 1895.

Uniforms and weapons

The *Gendarmes Maures*, raised as early as 1831 to act as guides and scouts for the French military forces operating in Algeria, were in many aspects the precursors of the Spahis. They were uniformed in the local fashion of their homeland: light blue vest in Moorish style, red *gilet* without buttons on the front, light blue loose trousers, red waist-sash, red *calotte* cap with white turban and light blue *burnous* cloak worn over another white one. This attire was used together with Arab boots and Moorish horse equipment. Both the *veste* and the *gilet* were trimmed with black lace; the former had decorative black embroiderings in the form of an S-shaped knot on each side of the front. The pointed cuffs had black piping. Weapon-

French officer of the Algerian Spahis with M1841 "European" uniform.

ry consisted of the M1822 flintlock infantry musket, M1822 light cavalry sabre and a couple of locally-manufactured flintlock pistols carried inside a holster made of red leather. The Algerian auxiliary cavalrymen serving alongside the African Chasseurs received some sort of uniform in 1831, shortly after their formation. This consisted of the following elements: *garance* red vest in Moorish style, light blue *gilet* without buttons on the front, light blue loose trousers, *amarante* red waist-sash, scarlet red *calotte* cap with *amarante* red turban and medium green *burnous* cloak. This attire, of clear Algerian fashion, was used together with Arab boots and Moorish horse equipment. The French officers of the Algerian auxiliary cavalrymen were dressed like the men under their command, but had additional decorative embroidery on the front and on the sleeves of their vests; these were mostly black, but could also be golden. Rank was shown by inverted *chevrons* applied above the pointed cuffs of the *veste*; these were yellow for NCOs and gold for officers. In 1834, with the first regularization of the Spahis, the colour of the *burnous* was changed from medium green to *garance*. Originally the vest worn by troopers was quite simple, being trimmed on the external edges with black lace. By 1841, however, it was decorated on the front with two S-shaped black knots almost identical to those of the Zouaves' uniform. With the progression of time the light blue *gilet* also started to be trimmed in black. On 7 December 1841, with the final regularization of the Spahis, the existing uniform was slightly modified: the red *burnous* started to be worn over a white *burnous*, while the red *chéchia* or *calotte* started to be produced in two different versions. The first, worn by French soldiers, had a light blue tassel and a white turban with light blue vertical stripes; the second, worn by Algerian soldiers, did not have the tassel and was covered with a white *haik*. The latter was different from a standard turban, since it was a larger piece of cloth that covered both the head and the shoulders; it was kept in position around the head by hard strips of camel skin. With the dress regulations of 7 December 1841 the rankers and native officers retained more or less their previous dress, while the French officers were given a new uniform of European cut. This consisted of the following elements: light blue *képi* with red bottom band and golden quarter-piping showing rank; *garance* red *spencer* (short jacket) with black trimming to the front and bottom edges as well as seven rows of black frogging; light blue trousers with large red side-stripe. The collar of the *spencer* was red with black piping; the pointed cuffs were light blue with black piping; rank was shown on the sleeves by golden Hungarian knots. The latter, since 1842, started to also be worn by the native officers instead of the previous inverted *chevrons*. Trumpeters were dressed like troopers, but with light blue *veste* and *garance* red trousers. Weaponry and equipment of troopers consisted of one ammunition pouch made of red leather, one holster made of red leather with two flintlock pistols inside, M1822 light cavalry sabre (often replaced with a locally-manufactured Arab sabre) and M1822 flintlock artillery musketoon. In 1858 new dress regulations were promulgated for the Spahis. These did not modify in a significant way the previous ones of 1841 and remained valid until 1914. The uniform of rankers was as

Trooper of the Algerian Spahis fighting in Crimea.

follows: *garance* red *chéchia* having light blue tassel and being worn with white turban having light blue vertical stripes for French troopers or *garance* red *chéchia* worn under white *haik* fastened with stripes of camel skin for Algerian troopers; *garance* red *veste* with light blue pointed cuffs piped in black, light blue piping to the edges, black trimming and black S-shaped knots on the front having their bottom loop (known as *tombò*) in the distinctive colour of each unit (light blue for the 1st Regiment, *jonquille* yellow for the 2nd Regiment and *garance* red for the 3rd Regiment); light blue *gilet* with black frontal trimming; light blue loose trousers with side pockets trimmed in black; crimson waist-sash; *garance* red *burnous* worn over another white one. The uniform used by French officers did not change from the 1841 dress regulations except for the *képi* that became smaller and entirely light blue. According to the 1858 dress regulations, the native officers of the Spahis were dressed like the men under their command but with golden Hungarian knots on the sleeves of their *veste*. NCOs' rank was shown by yellow inverted *chevrons* applied above the pointed cuffs, while the years of service of both NCOs and rankers was shown by golden inverted *chevrons* applied on the left sleeve. Trumpeters continued to wear uniforms with reversed colours. Note that the white *haik* was worn over the *chéchia* and fastened with strips of camel skin. The Tunisian Spahis, raised in 1886, were uniformed exactly like the Algerian ones. Their regimental colour, shown in the *tombò*, was black. In order to mount more easily on their horses, the Spahis could fold up their white *burnous* and suspend it with a white cord that was attached to the waistbelt. With the French Army's new dress regulations of 1873 the French officers of the Spahis replaced their previous uniform with a new light blue one that closely resembled that worn by the metropolitan light cavalry: *garance* red *képi* with light blue bottom band and golden quarter-piping showing rank; light blue *dolman* with red collar piped in black, light blue pointed cuffs piped in black, three vertical rows with nine golden buttons each on the front, nine horizontal rows of black frogging, black trimming to the front and bottom edges, golden Hungarian knots on the sleeves and golden shoulder knots showing rank; *garance* red tight trousers with light blue double side-stripes. During the French expedition to Tonkin (1883–1886) the Spahis wore their standard uniform but replaced their usual headgear with the white *casque coloniale*. In 1899 the French officers of the Spahis, like those of the African Chasseurs, adopted the same M1892 single-breasted short tunic that had been introduced for the French light cavalry. This – being red for the Spahis – had a single row of seven buttons on the front and a standing collar; being quite simple, it was worn for parade but also on campaign. The evolution of the Spahis' weaponry followed that of the *Chasseurs d'Afrique*. The M1822 flintlock artillery musketoon was replaced with the M1822t dragoon musket, this was in turn replaced with the M1842 percussion dragoon musket by the outbreak of the Crimean War. After receiving the M1860 dragoon musket, the Spahis adopted the M1866 Chassepot cavalry carbine and the M1874 Grass cavalry carbine. Finally they received the M1890 Lebel cavalry carbine, which they also used during World War I. The two pistols, albeit more and more sporadically, continued to be used until 1860.

French officer of the Algerian Spahis wearing M1873 uniform.

French NCO (left) and native trooper (right) of the Algerian Spahis in 1876.

Above, left: Native officer of the 3rd Regiment of Algerian Spahis in parade dress, 1900. ASKB

Above, right: French NCO of the 1st Regiment of Algerian Spahis in parade dress, 1900.

Native trooper of the 1st Regiment of Algerian Spahis in parade dress, 1900. ASKB

Above, left: Native trooper of the 1st Regiment of Algerian Spahis in parade dress, 1900.

Above, right: French NCO of the 1st Regiment of Algerian Spahis in campaign dress, 1900. The headgear is worn without turban. ASKB

Native trumpeter of the 2nd Regiment of Algerian Spahis, 1900. ASKB

Native trooper (left) and NCO (right) of the 2nd Regiment of Algerian Spahis in 1910.

Algerian Spahis on a reconnaissance mission during the early years of the 20th century. ASKB

Trooper of the "Gendarmes Maures" from the end of the 19th century. The "Gendarmes Maures" continued to exist as a para-military police corps after the creation of the Algerian Spahis. With the progression of time, the main colour of their uniform changed from light blue to black. ASKB

Trooper of the Algerian Spahis photographed in France at the beginning of the Great War.

The Bataillons d'infanterie légère d'Afrique

History and organization

The Battalions of African Light infantry were created on 13 June 1832 as a sort of semi-penal military corps. Their rankers, in fact, were chosen from soldiers of the metropolitan army who had been condemned to correctional penalties or from civilian convicts who, upon completing their terms of imprisonment, still had to meet their obligations for compulsory military service. Since 1818 the French Army had included some "disciplinary companies" of fusiliers or sappers, but these had been mostly employed as auxiliary corps and not as combat units. The French authorities, in fact, were worried about the idea of arming the *rabistes* or "hungry men" who had been punished by military justice. With the conquest of Algiers, these ex-deserters or undisciplined soldiers had an opportunity to fight again for their country but away from their homeland.

The African Light Infantry initially consisted of two battalions with eight companies each (increased to ten in 1834), which were sent to Tataouine on the border between Algeria and Tunisia. This was one of the most arid and hostile places of North Africa, where no regular soldier wanted to serve. Once in Algeria, the members of the African Light Infantry earned their nickname of "*Les Joyeux*" or "The Happy Ones"; they were, in fact, not particularly enthusiastic about their new life in North Africa. In September 1833 a 3rd *Bataillon d'infanterie légère d'Afrique* was formed and from 1836 civilian convicts who had completed their period of compulsory military service also started to be admitted into the ranks of the African Light Infantry. Initially the three battalions were mostly employed as auxiliary units of sappers, but several of their companies later took part in some combat operations. The 10th Company of the 1st Battalion, in particular, distinguished itself in 1840 during the Battle of Mazagran. The latter saw *Les Joyeux* defending their positions with great courage from the assaults of 1,200 Algerian fighters loyal to Abd al-Qādir.

During the Crimean War two temporary companies of African Light Infantry, made up of volunteers coming from the three existing battalions, participated in the hostilities. In 1860 the 3rd Battalion was sent to China, while the 2nd Battalion took part in the Mexican Adventure. With the outbreak of the Franco-Prussian War, each of the three battalions provided two of its companies for the formation of a *Bataillon de Marche* that fought with distinction against the Prussians. During 1885–1889 the 3rd Battalion of African Light Infantry served in the Far East. Meanwhile, on 27 February 1889, another two battalions of *infanterie légère d'Afrique* were raised. The 4th Battalion garrisoned Tunisia, while the 5th Battalion garrisoned the border between Algeria and Morocco.

Officer (left) and private (right) of the African Light Infantry in 1832. ASKB

Uniforms and weapons

The battalions of African Light Infantry, created in 1831, were dressed and equipped like the infantrymen of the Foreign Legion during the whole period covered and thus their uniforms followed the general evolution of the French line infantry's dress. Their distinctive facing colour, which remained the same, was *joinquille* yellow. Upon their formation the units of African Light Infantry were dressed with black M1825 shako, dark blue M1828 *habit* (long-tailed coat) and *garance* red M1829 trousers. The headgear had yellow top band, tricolour national cockade, pompom in company colour, black leather visor, brass frontal plate and chinscale. The coat had collar, round cuffs, cuff flaps, *contre-epaulettes*, vertical pockets and front piped in yellow. The buttons of the *habit* were brass, while the turnbacks were yellow. Soon after their creation, however, the battalions of African Light Infantry replaced their uncomfortable shako with the M1833 *casquette d'Afrique* that was *garance* red with dark blue bottom band and piping. On most occasions, especially on campaign, the soldiers replaced their *habit* with the grey *capote* (greatcoat); this had yellow collar patches and was usually worn together with a black oilskin cover for the *casquette d'Afrique*. A new version of the latter, having a slightly different shape, was introduced in 1842. The dress regulations of 29 April 1845 introduced a new and long-skirted dark blue tunic or *tunique*, which was also adopted by the African Light Infantry. This – single breasted – had yellow piping to collar, round cuffs, cuffs flaps, front and *contre-epaulettes*. Together with the *tunique*, the dress regulations of 1845 also introduced a new model of grey *capote*; this, double-breasted like the previous one, had yellow collar patches and shoulder straps. The dress regulations of January 1858 modified the M1845 *tunique* by reducing the length of its skirt in a sensible way. Meanwhile, on 17 January 1850, the *casquette d'Afrique* was replaced with a new kind of headgear that later became known as M1852 *képi*. This had the same colours as the *casquette d'Afrique* but was much smaller than the latter. On 30 March 1852 green fringed *epaulettes* with red crescents were added on the shoulders of the tunic. The greatcoat was also modified in 1852, becoming dark blue. It received the same *epaulettes* as the tunic and started to be worn with the long skirt folded up on each side. In 1858 a new *képi*, smaller than the previous one, came into use. With the dress regulations of 30 March 1860 the French line infantry, and thus also the African Light Infantry, received a new dark blue *habit* known as a *basquine*. This was single-breasted and quite short. It had yellow collar and red piping to front, bottom edge, round cuffs and cuff flaps. The *epaulettes* did not change. In 1867 the uniform of the French line infantry was changed again, with the introduction of a dark blue double-breasted tunic having two rows of seven brass buttons on the front. This had yellow collar patches and yellow piping to the front and pointed cuffs for the African Light Infantry, on the shoulders it had red *epaulettes* with green crescents and fringes. With the dress regulations of 1867 a new model of greatcoat was issued. This, double-breasted and with folded-up skirt, had yellow collar patches and red *epaulettes* with green crescents and fringes for the battalions of African Light Infantry. During the whole period described here, the latter were always equipped with the standard flintlock and percussion muskets of the French line infantry until the adoption of the M1866 Chassepot rifle. In 1873 the French line infantry and thus also the African Light Infantry received a new model of *képi*, having a slightly tapered and forward-pointing shape. Their M1867 tunic, instead, continued to be worn until 1897 and was only slightly modified during the period 1867–1897. The new M1897 tunic was used until 1914 as parade dress. This had red collar with brass battalion number, red cuff flaps, red piping to the round cuffs and green *epaulettes* having red crescents and green fringes. Since their foundation in 1831, the battalions of African Light Infantry wore *garance* red trousers like the metropolitan line infantry. Their NCO's rank was always shown by yellow stripes like the ones worn by our corporal. These were also applied on the greatcoat, which was of general use on campaign. In 1877 the M1867 *capote* was slightly modified and assumed the features that it would retain until 1914. Like the previous one, this was dark blue and double breasted with a red collar patch bearing the battalion number for the African Light Infantry. In 1884 a new model of *képi* was introduced and this, having dark blue bottom band and quarter piping, remained in use until 1914. In 1876 the battalions of African Light Infantry replaced their Chassepots with the M1874 Gras rifle, which remained in use until 1886. Subsequently they received the new M1886 Lebel rifle that remained in use until 1914.

Privates of the African Light Infantry with M1845 uniforms; the figures on the left are wearing working dress, while the figure on the right is wearing campaign dress.

Private of the African Light Infantry with M1845 greatcoat.

Private of the 1st Battalion of African Light Infantry in 1900.

The Saharan units

History and organization

In 1843 the French military authorities in Algeria formed a first "experimental" corps of infantrymen mounted on dromedaries. This initially consisted of just 40 volunteers taken from the 33rd Regiment of Line Infantry and was later expanded to become a company with 100 men (volunteers taken from the 33rd Regiment of Line Infantry and 3rd Battalion of Light Infantry). This early camel corps, which received an official organization in January 1844, was also given two mountain howitzers. During 1848, however, it was disbanded following the defeat of Abd al-Qādir. During the military emergency of 1871–1872, caused by the Algerian uprising, some companies of Tirailleurs were temporarily mounted on dromedaries. Later, in 1885, an experimental corps mounted on mules was created. This, very short-lived, unit consisted of 250 volunteers organized into four "sections". Each pair of soldiers had a mule and the latter was used to transport the personal equipment of both men. One soldier marched and the other rode the mule, every hour the two men exchanged their position in order to give some rest to the one who had been marching. This other experimental corps, however, was also very short-lived.

Following their conquest of Saharan Algeria, in order to patrol the vast desert areas of the south and to keep order among the nomadic Tuaregs, the French decided to create their first "Saharan" military units in 1894. These consisted of three infantry companies of Saharan Tirailleurs and three cavalry platoons of Saharan Spahis (the latter making up a single squadron). These were recruited from the Arab Chaamba tribe, which had been fighting against the Tuaregs for centuries, but were not *méhariste* or camel-mounted troops (the Arab word *mehari* was used to indicate the dromedaries of the Sahara). In 1897 François-Henry Laperrine, a military officer but also an explorer of the Sahara Desert, was appointed commander of the Saharan Spahis. Very soon he understood that his men, mounted on horses, were in no conditions to counter the Tuareg raiders in an effective way. As a result, in 1899 Laperrine presented to the French authorities a project for the formation of some new Saharan companies that had to be mounted on dromedaries. These would be recruited from the Chaamba tribe like the previous Saharan military units. On 30 March 1902 Laperrine's project was approved and the creation of five *Compagnies méharistes sahariennes* was authorized. Each of these (reduced to four in 1905) was based in a different oasis – Tassili, Tindouf, El Oued, Adrar and Tamanrasset. A single company consisted of one infantry platoon and three platoons mounted on dromedaries. It comprised the following elements: 6 French officers, 36 French NCOs or rankers and 300 native rankers. Each company also had two mountain howitzers of 80 mm. Thanks to their flexible organization and great mobility, the *Compagnies méharistes sahariennes* did not experience any logistic problem while operating in the Sahara Desert and could easily travel for 30 kilometres every day. They were the only units capable of intercepting the Tuaregs and thus played a fundamental role in securing French control over the land routes that connected Algeria with Senegal. The *Compagnies méharistes sahariennes* had their own independent commands but were part of the 19th Army Corps.

Uniforms and weapons

The Saharan Tirailleurs wore white *haik* with light brown strips of camel skin, black cloak worn over another white one, white blouse, red waist-sash, white *séroual* trousers and brown leather boots. The Saharan Spahis wore white *haik* with dark brown strips of camel skin, dark brown cloak worn over another white one, white blouse, red waist-sash, white *séroual* trousers and brown leather boots. Both the Saharan Tirailleurs and Saharan Spahis, on campaign, used the wide-brimmed *tarazala* straw hat that was extremely popular in southern Algeria and Tunisia. The bedouins who made up the companies of *Méharistes Sahariennes* were dressed with the traditional costume of the Tuaregs, the nomads of the Sahara. This consisted of white or black *chèche* (a large piece of cloth covering the head as a turban but also the throat and the neck), white *lithan* (the veil worn over the face), white *gandourah* or sleeveless light tunic worn over white undergarments and white *séroual* loose trousers. The *chèche* could be fastened around the head with dark brown or medium brown strips of camel skin. The French officers and NCOs of the *Méharistes Sahariennes* wore the same light blue *képi* with golden quarter piping and *garance* red single-breasted tunic used by their equivalents of the Spahis since 1899. They, however, wore the same *séroual* trousers and brown leather sandals used by the bedouin soldiers. The weapons and equipment of the Saharan units in French service were the same employed by the Tirailleurs and by the Spahis.

Above, left: Soldier of the experimental corps mounted on dromedaries that was raised in 1843; judging from his uniform, he is a grenadier of the 33rd Regiment of Line Infantry.

Above, right: Private of the Saharan Tirailleurs, with *tarazala* straw hat on the back.

Left: Private of the Saharan Tirailleurs.

Right: Trooper of the Saharan Spahis, with tarazala straw hat.

Soldier of the *Compagnies méharistes sahariennes* in 1904.

The Tunisian and Moroccan native units

History and organization

The first "westernized" Tunisian Army originated during the last months of 1830, following the French conquest of Algiers. Hussayn Bey (ruler of Tunisia), in fact, decided that a modern army had to be organized in his country as soon as possible in order to face an eventual French attack against Tunis. By 1832 the small Tunisian Army consisted of two line infantry regiments with two battalions each. In 1837 a 3rd Infantry Regiment was created but an early attempt to introduce military conscription failed completely. In 1838 a cavalry regiment, equipped with lances, and an artillery regiment were formed. In 1840 a first Military School was established at Bardo, in 1842 another three infantry regiments were raised from conscripts and in 1846 another artillery regiment was created. From 1843 a French military mission was active in Tunisia, but its instructors did not improve in a significant way the general quality of the local military units. The recruiting system remained of the most haphazard nature, since conscripts were impressed to serve only when some new corps had to be raised. By 1847 the Tunisian Army consisted of the following units: 7 regiments of line infantry with three battalions of eight companies each, 1 regiment of cavalry with four squadrons and 2 regiments of artillery with three battalions of eight companies each. In addition to the above there were a regiment of naval infantry, a small mounted "Bey's Bodyguard", three corps of *Spahis* irregular cavalry and several auxiliary foot units recruited from the warlike Zwawa tribes (the latter had always provided some excellent soldiers to the authorities of Tunis). During 1848–1853 another two regiments of artillery were formed and in addition both the regiments of infantry and those of artillery started to be known as "brigades" despite retaining their previous internal organization. The Tunisian expeditionary force that took part to the Crimean War consisted of 7,000 men: six infantry battalions, one cavalry regiment and two field batteries with six guns each. In 1860 the Tunisian Army was reduced to six regiments of infantry, one squadron of cavalry and one regiment of artillery. During that same year a new conscription law was promulgated, according to which a drafted conscript was to serve for a period of eight years. In 1881, shortly before France's conquest of Tunisia, the structure of the army was almost the same as in 1860: seven regiments of infantry, one squadron of cavalry and four battalions of artillery.

Until the 1860s the Sultanate of Morocco did not have an army organized according to "modern" European principles, since its military forces were structured according to a tribal system that dated back to the late 17th century. The various Moroccan tribes were divided into two main categories, the *maghzen* and the *nouaib*. The former were "military tribes" that were tasked with providing the warriors needed by the Sultan to garrison the major cities and to form the semi-permanent central army; the latter were "ordinary tribes" that were asked to provide warriors only in case of full mobilization for war. There were four *maghzen* tribes, famous for their loyalty towards the Sultan – *Oudaia*, *Cheraga*, *Cherarda* and *Bouakhar*. Each of them was to provide a certain number of soldiers (both infantrymen and cavalrymen) serving on a permanent basis (known as *raha*) and a certain number of soldiers acting as "reserve troops". The *maghzen* warriors were all organized into standard units with 500 men each. Around 1860 these were the contingents provided by each tribe: 1,500 permanent soldiers and 2,000 reservists for *Oudaia*, 2,500 permanent soldiers and 4,000 reservists for *Cheraga*, 3,500 permanent soldiers for *Cherarda* and 4,000 reservists for *Bouakhar*. In addition to these there was the Guard of the Sultan or *Abad*, which was formed at the beginning of the 18th century and initially consisted of 14,000 black slaves bought from Senegal and Sudan. In 1727 most of the original black slaves/soldiers were incorporated into the *maghzen* tribe of the *Bouakhar*, but a Guard of the Sultan also continued to exist during the following decades (which still consisted of trusted black soldiers). Following the Spanish-Moroccan War of 1859–1860, during which the tribal military forces of the Sultanate were utterly defeated, the Moroccans decided to re-organize their army along European lines and to "westernize" it. Zouave-style uniforms were introduced, modern weapons were bought from abroad and a regular "central" army was progressively organized. At the beginning of the 20th century the new Moroccan Army consisted of the following units: 30 battalions of infantry, 1 corps of cavalry, 2 battalions of artillery and 1 corps of engineers. Each infantry battalion or *tabor* consisted of five companies with 100 men each. The latter could be members of the *maghzen* tribes or volunteers coming from the *nouaib* tribes. The Moroccan regular infantry was equipped with a variety of different rifles, the most common of which was the French Gras. The Martini-Henry, Remington and Winchester rifles were also quite popular. The cavalry, raised only in 1903, was very small and consisted of just 700 troopers since the bulk of the Sultanate's mounted troops continued to be provided by the "military tribes". The two battalions of artillery had seven batteries/companies each, six of mountain artillery and one of horse artillery. The artillerymen were all volunteers and were trained by French instructors. Most of their pieces were M1895 Krupp mountain guns of 75mm that were transported on mules. The engineers consisted of just a few officers who had studied in France. Before Morocco became a protectorate of France, the Guard of the Sultan consisted of two autonomous branches, the "Interior Guard" and the "Exterior Guard". The first comprised 1,250 soldiers (310 mounted) and the second had 3,500 cavalrymen (500 of whom were tasked with delivering the orders of the Sultan to the various tribes).

From 1907 the Army of Africa started to campaign in Morocco, having as its main objective that of transforming the latter country into a French protectorate. Very soon the French military commanders felt the need for some locally-recruited contingents of auxiliaries, who could act as guides and interpreters for their own columns. The French troops, in fact, did not have a proper knowledge of Morocco's interior areas and thus frequently ran the risk of being ambushed by the nomadic fighters of the local resistance forces. As a result of the above situation, on 9 September 1908 a first *goum* or company was recruited by the French from Moroccan individuals who wanted to serve under their flag. The Arab term *gum*, transformed into *goum* by the French, was used to indicate the contingents that each Moroccan tribe had to provide to the central government of the Sultanate. The members of this new corps soon started to be known as *Goumiers*. The French military authorities had a very good impression of these irregular Moroccan soldiers and thus – on 30 November 1908 – they decided to organize six *goums* with 200 men each. The latter were mixed units of infantry and cavalry, since they consisted of 150 infantrymen and 50 cavalrymen. Basically, the *Goumiers* were tribal fighters since they had a semi-regular nature at best and did not wear uniforms. They, however, were very important for the French and proved to be effective mountain fighters in the harsh terrain of the Moroccan Atlas. Each *goum* was given French officers and some Algerian NCOs, in order to acquire a more regular status. In addition to the semi-regular *Goumiers*, the French also recruited several irregular bands of infantrymen and cavalrymen. These, together with the six semi-regular *goums*, made up the so-called *Troupes auxiliaries Marocaines* or Moroccan Auxiliary Troops. In 1912 the number of *goums* was increased from 6 to 12 and four of the latter (the 5th, 6th, 11th and 12th) were grouped together in order to form the nucleus for a first unit of Moroccan regular infantry. On 9 April 1913 the *Goumiers* officially became part of the Army of Africa, after having shown their valour in combat during the years 1911–1912. In 1913 the French authorities worked hard to create the first regular infantry units made up of Moroccans, which became known as *Chasseurs indigènes à pied* or Native Foot Chasseurs and – by the outbreak of World War I – consisted of five independent *tabors* or battalions with four companies each. In August 1914, with the war mobilization, these were assembled into two regiments (the first with three battalions and the second with two battalions) that made up the new *Brigade de chasseurs indigènes*. In August 1914 the French also organized their first regular cavalry unit made up of Moroccans, by assembling together the previous irregular corps of auxiliary horsemen into a *Régiment de Marche de Chasseurs indigènes à cheval*. The latter, despite being a temporary corps, was not disbanded after the end of the hostilities and in 1920 it became the 1st Regiment of Moroccan Spahis. The *Brigade de chasseurs indigènes*, instead, was transformed into a single regiment during 1915 and became the 1st Regiment of Moroccan Tirailleurs in 1918. Following the transformation of Morocco into a protectorate of France, the Moroccan Army was disbanded and most of its members became part of the new regular units raised by the French as part of the Army of Africa. Only the Guard of the Sultan was not disbanded and it assumed the new denomination of *Garde Chérifienne* and was re-structured by the French in 1912. From the latter year it consisted of 500 men (all blacks) assembled into three companies of infantry, one squadron of cavalry and one battery of artillery.

Uniforms and weapons

The Tunisian contingent that participated to the Crimean War was still dressed with the uniform introduced in 1830–1831. For the infantry this consisted of a red *tarboosh* headgear with black tassel, dark blue single-breasted jacket with red collar and pointed cuffs, entirely dark blue trousers. The artillery was uniformed like the infantry, but with a yellow flaming grenade embroidered on the front of the headgear. The naval infantry had a yellow anchor embroidered on the front of the *tarboosh*. The cavalry wore a dark blue jacket with three vertical rows of buttons on the front. White jackets and trousers were of common use during hot months. In 1881, shortly before being disbanded by the French, the Tunisian Army adopted new uniforms that were clearly influenced by those of the contemporary *Armée d'Afrique*. These, for all branches of service, consisted of the following elements: red *chéchia* with black tassel, dark blue vest with red embroidery and trimming having red piping to pointed cuffs, dark blue waistcoat with red trimming, red waist-sash and white loose trousers. During hot months an entirely white version of this same dress was used. The Guard of the Beylik – which comprised sub-units of infantry, cavalry and artillery – was uniformed since its formation very similarly to the French Zouaves. The red *chéchia* had dark blue tassel and a brass frontal badge reproducing the coat-of-arms of the Beylikate of Tunis. The dark blue vest had red embroidery and trimming. Its pointed cuffs were piped in red and on the front it bore a red decorative badge consisting of a five-pointed star and a crescent. The waistcoat was dark blue with red trimming, the waist-sash was medium blue and the loose trousers were red. During hot months an entirely white version of this same dress (always with embroidery and trimming in red) was used.

The regular Moroccan troops already wore Zouave-style uniforms before their country was transformed into a protectorate of France. Their standard dress consisted of a red *chéchia* with white turban or white *haik* and dark blue tassel, dark blue vest with red embroidery and trimming, pointed cuffs in the distinctive colour of each branch of service (red for infantry, green for cavalry, yellow for artillery), red waistcoat with dark blue trimming, dark blue waist-sash and dark blue trousers (white during hot months). The elite *Garde Chérifienne* wore a distinctive uniform of red *chéchia* with white turban and light blue tassel, dark blue single-breasted short tunic with brass buttons and folded collar having patches in the distinctive colour of each branch of service, golden piping to the round cuffs and light blue trousers having decorative embroidery on each side in the branch of service's colour. During the period 1908–1914 the Moroccan Goumiers had a distinctive semi-regular status, since they were employed as auxiliaries by the French Army of Africa but were under the command – at least formally – of the Sultan of Morocco. As a result of their particular condition, they did not wear a proper uniform and were dressed with the traditional clothes of the Moroccan mountaineers living in the Atlas Mountains. These consisted

Above: Private of the Tunisian *Garde Beylicale* photographed in 1912. The Guard of the Beylik – which comprised sub-units of infantry, cavalry and artillery – was uniformed since its formation very similarly to the French Zouaves. The red *chéchia* had dark blue tassel and a brass frontal badge reproducing the coat-of-arms of the Beylikate of Tunis. The dark blue vest had red embroidering and trimming; its pointed cuffs were piped in red and on the front it bore a red decorative badge consisting of a five-pointed star and a crescent. The waistcoat was dark blue with red trimming, the waist-sash was medium blue and the loose trousers were red.

Above, right: Private (left) and NCO (right) of the Moroccan Army's infantry in 1912. The regular Moroccan troops wore Zouave-style uniforms already before their country was transformed into a protectorate of France. Their standard dress consisted of a red *chéchia* with white turban or white haik and dark blue tassel, dark blue vest with red embroidering and trimming, pointed cuffs in the distinctive colour of each branch of service (red for infantry, green for cavalry, yellow for artillery), red waistcoat with dark blue trimming, dark blue waist-sash and dark blue trousers (white during hot months).

Right: Officer (left) and private (right) of the Moroccan *Goumiers* photographed in 1914. They are both wearing white *chéchia*, striped djellaba and brown *séroual* trousers. The puttees, shoes, ammunition pouches and Lebel rifle are all French.

of four main elements: the *chéchia* headgear, the *djellaba* outer robe, the *séroual* trousers and the *babouche* slippers. The Moroccan *chéchia* was taller than that used by the Algerian or Tunisian Tirailleurs; most of the Goumiers had it in red and without tassel. The *djellaba* is a long and loose-fitting outer robe, hooded and with full sleeves; made of wool, it is perfect for the extreme temperatures of the Sahara Desert. The *djellaba* could be coloured in many different shades of brown and, in most cases, it was decorated with vertical stripes in contrasting colours. According to some contemporary sources, each *tabor* or battalion of Goumiers had its own distinctive colours for the *djellaba*. The *séroual* trousers were extremely large and were usually white; the *babouche* slippers, instead, were made of brown leather and were perfect to walk for long periods on mountain terrain. The first two regiments of Moroccan Tirailleurs were organized only in August 1914, by transforming the *Troupes auxiliaries Marocaines* into regular units. As a result, until the early months of World War I, the Moroccan Tirailleurs continued to be dressed with a semi-regular dress. This was very similar to that worn by the Goumiers and comprised red *chéchia*, brown *djellaba* and *séroual* trousers. The *djellaba*, which could have some coloured edging on the front, was worn over a *vareuse* or short blouse that was closed on the front by seven brass buttons. The *séroual* trousers could be tucked into French dark blue puttees (called *chiffoun* by the Moroccan soldiers) and the tribal *babouche* slippers could be replaced with European black shoes. The black ammunition pouches, provided by the French, were the standard ones for the M1886 Lebel rifle, but the knapsack, instead, was of the so-called *barda* type produced in Morocco. This had shoulder straps made of cord and was cylindrical in shape. The Moroccan Spahis were organized into a first regular regiment only after the outbreak of World War I. Until then they were part of the *Troupes auxiliaries Marocaines* and wore the following semi-regular uniform: white *chèche*, *garance* red short *veste* with a single row of seven leather buttons on the front having light blue folded collar and round cuffs, light blue *séroual* trousers without decorative embroidery on the side pockets, scarlet red waist-sash made of wool, *garance* red *burnous* cloak worn over another white one. The weapons and equipment of the Tunisian and Moroccan units in French service were the same employed by the Tirailleurs and by the Spahis.

The Naval and Colonial Troops, 1815–1914

Since the last decades of the 17th century the colonial military forces of France had been placed under the control of the navy and not of the army. Each of the overseas territories, in fact, had an autonomous administration but its military forces were raised and supplied by the Ministry of the Navy. The fact that the troops serving in the overseas colonies should be placed under the control of the navy was something quite logical for the time, since the colonial troops had to be transported and supplied to the other continents by France's naval forces. Initially the French colonial troops, created by Louis XIV and by his visionary minister Jean-Baptiste Colbert, consisted of just a few independent infantry companies – known as "*Compagnies franches de la Marine*" or "Independent Naval companies" – which started to be despatched to French Canada from 1683 in order to act as the garrison of the vast American colony, as well as to play an important role in the colonization of the latter. Until the outbreak of the Seven Years' War in 1756 the system based on the "*Compagnies franches de la Marine*" worked quite well, but after both Canada and most of the colonial outposts in India were lost to the British in 1763 the French troops serving overseas had to be completely reformed. Since the soldiers of the metropolitan army were not willing to serve outside France – mostly because the colonies were characterized by a hostile natural environment in which tropical diseases were quite common – the independent "*Troupes de la Marine*" or "Naval Troops" were retained in service but began to consist of larger units (regiments, battalions or mixed "legions" that comprised elements of cavalry and artillery in addition to infantry). Each of the overseas territories was assigned one or more of such new corps, in addition to a variable number of independent colonial artillery companies. The latter were mostly tasked with garrisoning the fortifications of the various territories and thus had a quite static nature. The "*Troupes de la Marine*", be they infantry or artillery corps, were raised and paid by the French Navy but had autonomous commands. In addition, they were not part of the Naval Infantry and Naval Artillery corps of the French Navy that performed completely different tasks (i.e. providing the French warships with marines/naval gunners and garrisoning the French Navy's bases in metropolitan France). It should be noted, however, that on several occasions some detachments of Naval Infantry or Naval Artillery supported the "*Troupes de la Marine*" when needed since they were the only kind of reinforcements that the central government could supply quite rapidly to the military forces serving overseas. The "*Troupes de la Marine*" were recruited from volunteers who were interested in settling overseas and thus mostly consisted of men who had little to lose in France.

Unlike those of the metropolitan army, who were all aristocrats coming from the noble families of France, the officers of the colonial units could come from the lowest ranks of society and earned their positions thanks to their personal abilities. The "*Troupes de la Marine*", in addition, also comprised some locally-raised corps of "natives" who were recruited from the friendly communities living in the French overseas possessions. Already during the first half of the 18th century, for example, the colonial troops of French India included significant numbers of local professional soldiers who were known as "*Cipahis*" (the French equivalents of the British "Sepoys").

Being a separate entity from both the metropolitan army and the naval infantry/artillery corps, the Colonial Troops did not follow the latter's orders on structure of the units, uniforms, pay, equipment and awards. Since Louis XIV's days, the Ministry of the Navy was fully responsible for the administration of the various colonies and thus it gradually started to have its own autonomous army that was tasked with garrisoning an empire that comprised overseas possessions located in all the continents. After the outbreak of the French Revolution, especially during the Napoleonic Period, the French government attempted to absorb the Colonial Troops into the metropolitan army but this

Private of the 88th Departmental Legion serving in Martinique, 1815.

"experiment" led to negative results. The "*Troupes de la Marine*", in fact, had specific needs that could not be understood in Paris and were proud of their own peculiarities. A vast colonial empire like the French one could be administered – at least from a military point of view – only by having a separate body of troops specifically tasked with serving overseas on a permanent basis.

The naval and colonial troops of 1815–1830

When the Revolution broke out in 1789, France had several colonies spread over three continents. These possessions were not vast in territory, but their economic importance was great and thus they were often envied by the other major European powers. Nearly all the French colonies owed their wealth to exploitation of local resources by slave labour and to commerce. During the Napoleonic Wars most of them were temporarily occupied by the British, who could count on the superiority of their Royal Navy to isolate and attack the French overseas possessions (which rarely received any reinforcements and supplies). With the loss of Haiti, which became an independent republic in 1803 thanks to British help, these were France's remaining colonies in 1815 when the Bourbon royal family was restored on the French throne by the powers that had won the Napoleonic Wars: Martinique, Guadeloupe and some other smaller islands in the Caribbean area; Guyana on the northern coastline of South America; Isle-de-France and Isle-de-Bourbon in the Indian Ocean; the city of Pondichéry in India; Senegal in Africa and Saint-Pierre-et-Miquelon in the Atlantic Ocean. During the Napoleonic Wars, especially after most of the French Navy's vessels were destroyed at the Battle of Trafalgar in 1805, France's colonies were attacked and conquered one-by-one by the Royal

Voltigeur (light infantryman) of the Battalions of the Colonies, 1816.

Fusilier of the Battalion of Guyana, 1816.

Navy except for a few ones. As a result the French colonial forces, which Napoleon had tried to re-structure but without success, were almost non-existent by the end of the Napoleonic Wars and thus had to be re-built practically from zero.

In 1814, following the first abdication of Napoleon, the restored Bourbons decided that their colonial possessions would have been garrisoned by detachments of the metropolitan army's infantry units. One battalion of the 26th Line Infantry Regiment was sent to Martinique, one battalion of the 42nd Line Infantry Regiment was sent to Guadeloupe, two companies of the 73rd Line Infantry Regiment were sent to Guyana and one battalion of the 5th Light Infantry Regiment was sent to Isle-de-Bourbon. In addition, it was decided to create a new "*Régiment colonial étranger*" or "Foreign Colonial Regiment" by assembling together some of the many foreigners who had been part of the French Army under Napoleon's rule (mostly Spaniards from "Joseph Napoleon Regiment" and Portuguese from the "Portuguese Legion"). This new corps, also known as "Hohenlohe Regiment" from the name of its commander, was never sent overseas and thus became a standard foreign unit of the metropolitan army. Some years later its members gave birth to the famous French Foreign Legion.

Following Napoleon's return from the Elba, during the Hundred Days, Great Britain re-occupied most of the French colonies quite easily. After Bonaparte's final defeat, however, the various overseas possessions were returned to France. The Bourbons, following the military failures of the previous year, had to re-organize their colonial military forces again. In 1816 the royal government created a new system that was based on the co-existence of two different kinds of units: the "*Bataillons Coloniaux*" or "Colonial Battalions" and the "*Bataillons des Colonies*" or "Battalions of the Colonies". The first were penal military units, stationed in metropolitan France, which consisted of ex-deserters or of soldiers who had been punished for their indiscipline; the latter were proper colonial units, stationed in the overseas territories, which were made up of volunteers. The Battalions of the Colonies were to act as the garrisons of the various overseas possessions, while the Colonial Battalions were to act as their depots by providing new recruits to them. Some Colonial Battalions had already existed during the Napoleonic Period and thus their creation was not something completely new. The Bourbons raised three such units, each of which garrisoned a minor island of metropolitan France (Oléron, Hyères and Ré). By 1820, however, two of the battalions had been disbanded because of their indiscipline and the remaining one was transformed into a single "Penal Company" that lost its "colonial" status. During 1820 a new single Colonial Battalion was created at Rochefort to contin-

Private of the Colonial Battalions, 1816.

Grenadier of the Hohenlohe Regiment, 1824.

ue providing recruits for the Battalions of the Colonies, but this unit was also extremely short-lived and was disbanded in 1824. The Battalions of the Colonies created in 1816 and serving overseas were five and each of them was stationed in one of the following colonies: Martinique, Guadeloupe, Guyana, Isle-de-Bourbon and Senegal.

Following the second restoration of the Bourbons in 1815, the French infantry was reorganized in "Departmental Legions" and not in regiments. Each of these legions garrisoned a specific portion of the French territory and consisted of the following sub-units: two battalions of line infantry, one battalion of light infantry, one company of light cavalry and one company of artillery. Two of the new Departmental Legions were initially assigned to overseas service: the 88th Legion in Martinique and the 89th Legion in Guadeloupe. Very soon, however, these two larger units were transformed into normal Battalions of the Colonies like the other three garrisoning Guyana, Isle-de-Bourbon and Senegal. The Guyana Battalion was supported by a locally-raised corps, the "*Compagnie de Chasseurs Noirs de Cayenne*" or "Company of Cayenne's Black Chasseurs". This was a light infantry company made up of former black slaves who were mostly tasked with patrolling the French plantations located in Guyana's countryside and with crushing the frequent revolts of the local slave communities. Guyana, like several other European colonial possessions located in the Caribbean, had a large community of "maroons" or "runaway slaves" living in the forests of the interior areas and who frequently caused trouble to the French authorities

Gunners of the Naval Artillery with M1816 dress (left) and M1843 dress (right).

Officer and soldiers of the Naval Infantry with M1845 uniform.

that had to keep an eye on them. The Senegal Battalion was particularly unlucky since, while travelling to western Africa, the ship "*Méduse*" on which it was transported encountered a storm. The vessel was wrecked and half of its passengers died. In 1818 the Senegal Battalion, after replenishing its losses, was re-named 1st African Battalion; four years later, in 1822, it assumed the new denomination of Battalion of Gorée. In 1820 a new battalion was raised for service in Senegal, which was named 2nd African Battalion. The latter, in 1822, assumed the new denomination of Battalion of Senegal. The French colony of Pondichéry in India was not assigned any unit recruited in France, but from 1817 it was garrisoned by a single battalion of locally-raised Indian soldiers. These made up the so-called "Battalion of Cipahis", which consisted of four infantry companies that mostly performed police duties. All the new Battalions of the Colonies were not particularly effective, since they were made up of soldiers with little combat experience or who had experienced disciplinary problems. As a result, in order to improve the general quality of its colonial troops, in 1822 the French government decided to re-raise the Naval Infantry (which was no longer in existence since the early days of the Revolution) and to assign colonial military functions to it.

The history of the French Naval Infantry and Naval Artillery was quite complicated, especially during the Revolutionary and Napoleonic periods. On 26 December 1774, after some failed experiments, the French Navy reorganized its troops in 100 companies of naval infantry (collectively known as *Corps Royal d'Infanterie de la Marine*) and three companies of naval artillery (collectively known as *Bombardiers de la Marine*). These units usually acted independently from each other and served on the various warships of the fleet. A single company of naval infantry comprised the following elements: one lieutenant, two ensigns, one *fourrier*, six sergeants, six corporals, six lance-corporals, three drummers and 96 rankers. A single company of naval artillery comprised the following elements: two lieutenants, two ensigns, one *fourrier*, two sergeants, four

NCO of the Naval Infantry in Crimea, with M1852 uniform.

corporals, one drummer, 12 artificers and 50 bombardiers. In January 1786 the companies of naval infantry and naval artillery were assembled together to create a new *Corps royal des cannoniers-matelots* or "Royal Corps of gunners-sailors", which was the result of an attempt to consolidate the duties of the naval infantrymen/artillerymen with those of the sailors. The *cannoniers-matelots*, in fact, were trained in gunnery and in the use of small arms as well as in some aspects of the sailors' standard duties. The new corps was structured in nine "divisions", one for each of the nine squadrons that made up the French Navy at the time. A single division consisted of nine companies and the ratio of *cannoniers-matelots* embarked on warships was to be seven for every ten guns (for example, a 74-gun warship was to have about 52 such soldiers on board).

On 14 June 1792 the new republican government disbanded the *Corps royal des cannoniers-matelots* and, in its place, raised four regiments of naval infantry and two regiments of naval artillery (thus ending the "soldier-sailor" experiment). The four regiments of naval infantry had two battalions each and a single battalion consisted of eight "line" companies plus one "elite" company of grenadiers. The two regiments of naval artillery had two battalions each and a single battalion consisted of eight companies. In 1794 the French government decided to dissolve the naval infantry and naval artillery, but very soon it became apparent that this had been a great mistake and thus the formation of a new Marine Artillery Corps was decreed on 25 October 1795. This was to consist of seven "demi-brigades" or "half-brigades" with three battalions each, a single battalion comprising nine companies. The new "demi-brigades" were garrisoned in the major bases of the French Navy: three at Brest, one at Lorient, one at Rochefort and two at Toulon. According to the new organization, no marine infantry units were to be part of the French Navy since the naval artillerymen were to act also as naval infantrymen. On shore, for example,

Soldier of the Naval Infantry with M1852 uniform.

NCO (right) and officer (left) of the Naval Infantry wearing M1852 dress.

they had to garrison ports and naval arsenals. On 5 May 1803 Napoleon abolished the existing "demi-brigades" and consolidated them into four regiments. The first two of the latter had four battalions each, while the remaining two had just two battalions each. A single battalion consisted of six companies. The Marine Artillery Corps also comprised four companies of *ouvriers* or workers, which were augmented to six during 1805. By the latter year the four regiments of naval artillery were stationed at Brest, Rochefort, Lorient, Toulon and Genoa.

After the disastrous Russian Campaign of 1812, Napoleon had to re-build his military forces almost from zero and thus decided to employ his naval artillery regiments as normal line infantry units. On 24 January 1813 these were transferred from the Marine Department to the War Department and were reorganized as follows: the 1st Regiment in eight battalions, the 2nd Regiment in ten battalions, the 3rd Regiment in four battalions and the 4th Regiment in four battalions. A single battalion now consisted of six companies. Except for six of them that remained in the major ports, all the battalions of naval artillery were assembled together to create a "Marine Division" that fought brilliantly as line infantry during the German Campaign of 1813 and the French Campaign of 1814. The *ouvriers* had a different history: in 1806 they were expanded to two regiments that were recruited from men "without occupation", who were tasked with shipbuilding work as well as with garrison duties. During the following years another three such regiments were raised, but these units were all disbanded in June 1810. From 1808 a new militarized corps of marine workers had been formed, which initially consisted of just 18 companies and was later expanded to 8 battalions. This, known as *Ouvriers militaires de la Marine*, continued to exist until 1814 and took part in several military campaigns by providing "field" battalions.

With the second restoration of the Bourbons, in 1816, the surviving elements of the Marine Artillery Corps and of the *Ouvriers militaires de la Marine* were assembled together in order to form the new *Corps royal des cannoniers de la Marine* or "Royal Corps of Naval Artillerymen". The latter consisted of just eight battalions, which were tasked with providing the needed marines and naval gunners to the warships of the French Navy. On 7 August 1822, in view of the general reorganization of the colonial military forces, the Royal Corps of Naval Artillerymen was disbanded. After the failed experiments of the post-1815 years, the French military authorities finally understood that the difficult task of garrisoning the colonies could not be performed solely by Battalions of the Colonies recruited in France from volunteers of uncertain loyalty and little discipline. As a result, it was decided that both the Naval Infantry and the Naval Artillery would have to be re-created and that they would form the backbone of the Colonial Army (in addition to providing marines and naval gunners to the fleet as they had always done). On 13 November 1822 the Naval Infantry was organized in two regiments and the Naval Artillery in one regiment. The two regiments of naval infantry were to have three battalions each; a single marine battalion would consist of one company of grenadiers (heavy infantry), one company of *voltigeurs* (light infantry) and six companies of fusiliers. The regiment of naval artillery was to have 24 companies of naval gunners, 5 companies of cadet naval gunners and 5 companies of artillery workers. In addition the corps was to comprise several independent officers and NCOs who were to serve in the various French colonies in order to act as the "artillery staff" of the local garrisons. These detachments of naval artillery were supported by some locally-raised units of artillery workers, one company in Guyana and one company in Isle-de-Bourbon. In 1826 the five companies of cadet naval gunners were disbanded.

The naval infantry regiments created in 1822 also had to provide several detachments for service in the colonies, but this practice last for just a few years. The system based on the co-existence of naval infantry/artillery regiments and Battalions of the Colonies, in fact, was quite short-lived since the efficiency of the military units that were part of it was quite limited. The naval infantrymen, nicknamed "*marsouins*" or "porpoises" by the sailors because of their slowness of movement on the warships, were never particularly happy about the idea of serving far from France for long periods. The soldiers of the Battalions of the Colonies, nicknamed "*Les joyeux*" or "the happy ones" because of their frequent acts of insubordination, continued to be mostly recruited from individuals who had experienced disciplinary problems and thus were not particularly reliable. As a result of the above situation, in 1828, it was finally decided to disband the Battalions of the Colonies and to replace them with three regiments of the metropolitan army that would be tasked with serving overseas: the 45th Regiment of Line Infantry, the 51st Regiment of Line Infantry and the 16th Regiment of Light Infantry. Each of these was to consist of eight companies: seven of the latter would serve overseas and one would remain in France to act as depot. The regiments of naval infantry were disbanded in 1827, while the 24 companies of naval gunners and the 5 companies of artillery workers were retained in service. In 1829 the number of men in each company of the Naval Artillery Regiment was increased. The organizational measures introduced during 1827–1829 were clearly temporary ones, since a few scattered infantry companies from the metropolitan army were not enough to garrison the French overseas possessions in a proper way.

The naval and colonial troops of 1831–1870

On 14 May 1831, as a result of the French conquest of Algeria that took place during the previous year, it was decided to replace the companies of metropolitan infantry serving in the colonies with two new "*Régiments de la Marine*" or "Regiments of the Navy". Each of the latter was to consist of three battalions with eight companies: one company of grenadiers, one company of voltigeurs and six companies of fusiliers. The latter were later increased to eight, bringing the number of companies in each regiment to 30. The two new units, which would provide garrisons to all the French colonies, were to have a common depot in France (at Landerneau) consisting of six fusilier companies; in addition, they were to comprise a certain number of supernumerary officers and NCOs who would act as cadres for the formation of new locally-raised native units in the various colonies. On 20 November 1838 the 3rd Regiment of the Navy was formed. This replaced the depot companies of Landerneau and thus was not sent to serve overseas. It had a very large establishment comprising 30 companies: 4 of grenadiers, 4 of voltigeurs and 22 of fusiliers. According to the plans that led to its formation, the 3rd Regiment of the Navy was to act both as a depot for the other two existing regiments and as a sort of "reserve" to be used in case of need. Very soon, however, it started to be employed like the other two regiments. By 1838 the various companies of the three regiments were distributed as follows across the French territories: the 1st Regiment had 10 companies at Brest, 5 companies at Cherbourg and 15 companies on Guadeloupe; the 2nd Regiment had 5 companies at Brest, 10 companies at Rochefort and 15 companies in Martinique; the 3rd Regiment had 15 companies at Toulon, 6 companies in Guyana, 3 companies in Senegal and 6 companies in Isle-de-Bourbon. As regards the Naval Artillery Regiment, in 1835 the number of its gunner companies was reduced from 24 to 12; the latter were distributed as follows across the French territories: 4 companies at Lorient, 2 companies at Brest, 2 companies in Guadeloupe, 2 companies in Martinique, 1 company in Isle-de-Bourbon, 1 half-company in Guyana and 1 half-company in Senegal. In 1840, following the success of a punitive expedition mounted against Mexico, during which the naval artillerymen performed extremely well, the French government decided to increase the number of naval artillery companies first from 12 to 18 and then from 18 to 40. Most of the latter – 32 out of 40 – would be garrisoned in France to provide the needed detachments of marines/naval gunners to the fleet and thus only 8 companies would serve in the colonies. Until 1842 the Regiment of Naval Artillery also comprised 5 companies of workers, which were increased to 6 during that year. The new company, formed in 1842, was to provide detachments for the colonies.

In January 1842 the number of naval artillery companies was reduced from 40 to 30, with the disbandment of ten companies chosen from those serving in metropolitan France. During 1843, instead, the number of naval infantry companies from the Regiments of the Navy was increased following the occupation of some new colonial territories (Nosy Be and Mayotte near Madagascar, the Marquesas Islands in the Pacific). The number of companies in the 1st Regiment of the Navy and in the 3rd Regiment of the Navy was increased to 46, while in the 2nd Regiment of the Navy it was increased to 38. During this period the naval infantrymen provided most of the colonial garrisons, while the naval artillerymen – nicknamed "*bigors*" or "sea snails" because of their traditional static duties – acted as the marines and naval gunners for the warships of the

NCO of the Naval Infantry with M1873 parade dress.

NCO of the Naval Infantry with M1886 campaign dress, including tropical helmet made of cork and "paletot" double-breasted naval tunic.

fleet. Following the Revolution of 1848, France ceased to be a monarchy and became a republic. The great political changes of these years partly affected the organization of the colonial forces, but not in a very significant way. The three regiments of naval infantry had their establishments slightly reduced and deployed their companies as follows: the 1st Regiment had 14 companies at Brest, 21 companies at Guadeloupe and 6 companies in the Pacific; the 2nd Regiment had 10 companies at Rochefort, 9 companies at Cherbourg and 21 in Martinique; the 3rd Regiment had 13 companies at Toulon, 6 companies in Guyana, 6 companies in Senegal and 20 companies in Isle-de-Bourbon (the latter, since 1848, received the new republican denomination of La Réunion). The three regiments of naval infantry had their main bases in Guadeloupe, in Martinique and at Toulon. As for the Naval Artillery Regiment, in 1848 the number of its companies was reduced from 30 to 23. The latter were garrisoned as follows: 5 at Lorient, 4 at Brest, 2 at Cherbourg, 2 at Rochefort, 3 at Toulon, 2 in Martinique, 2 in Guadeloupe, 2 in La Réunion, 1 half-company in Guyana and 1 half-company in Senegal.

In 1852, following the proclamation of Napoleon III's Second Empire, the French colonial military forces entered in a new phase of their long history. The new Emperor, in fact, was strongly determined to expand the overseas possessions of his country by launching a series of new colonial campaigns. During 1852 Napoleon III ordered the disbandment of the grenadier and voltigeur companies existing in each regiment of naval infantry, but the number of men in the fusilier companies was increased and thus the overall strength of each regiment remained the same. On 31 August 1854 the naval infantry was completely reorganized, re-structured in four regiments having a variable number of battalions and came to comprise a total of 15,000 men assembled into a total of 120 companies. The 1st Regiment was to have four battalions with a total of 26 companies; the 2nd Regiment was to have six battalions with a total of 31 companies; the 3rd Regiment was to have four battalions with a total of 26 companies; the 4th Regiment was to have four battalions with a total of 27 companies. In 1856 an independent naval infantry battalion was created for providing detachments to the warships of the fleet, followed by a short-lived second one in 1861. After the end of the Crimean War, in 1856, the naval infantry companies were distributed as follows: the 1st Regiment had 18 companies at Cherbourg and 8 in Martinique; the 2nd Regiment had 22 companies at Brest, 8 in Guadeloupe and 4 in the Pacific; the 3rd Regiment had 17 companies at Rochefort and 9 in Guyana; the 4th Regiment had 22 companies at Toulon, 5 in La Réunion and 7 in Senegal. During 1857 the overall number of companies was slightly reduced from 120 to 118. During the Crimean War, on 5 June 1855, the Naval Artillery Regiment was re-organized into 25 companies of gunners and 6 companies of workers. In 1861 the number of naval artillery companies was increased to 28, garrisoned as follows: 7 at Lorient, 3 at Cherbourg, 2 at Brest, 2 at Rochefort, 3 at Toulon, 2 in Martinique, 2 in Guadeloupe, 1 in the Pacific, 1 full company and 1 half-company in Senegal, 1 in La Réunion, 1 in Cochinchina (Vietnam) and a half-company in Senegal.

Soldier of the volunteer infantry company from Martinique that participated to the Mexican Expedition of the 1860s. The uniform consists of dark blue kepi with red piping, dark blue jacket with red anchor badge on the collar and white trousers.

For the military expedition to Mexico (1861–1867), a single infantry company of volunteers was recruited from the black inhabitants of Martinique (who were accustomed to the Caribbean climate). In 1868 the naval infantry was expanded to comprise 140 companies, distributed as follows: the 1st Regiment had 17 companies at Cherbourg, 5 in Martinique, 5 in Senegal and 5 in Cochinchina; the 2nd Regiment had 21 companies at Brest, 5 in Guadeloupe and 10 in Cochinchina; the 3rd Regiment had 17 companies at Rochefort, 4 in La Réunion, 5 in Cochinchina, 5 in New Caledonia and 1 in Tahiti; the 4th Regiment had 21 companies at Toulon, 5 in Guyana, 11 in Cochinchina and 2 in the Pacific. The Regiment of Naval Artillery was not affected by any major organizational change and thus still consisted of 28 companies when the conflict between France and Prussia began in 1870.

The naval and colonial troops of 1871–1914

After the disastrous military defeats suffered during 1870–1871 in the Franco-Prussian War, France became again a republic and thus the Second Empire of Napoleon III came to an end. These important political changes led to a series of modifications in the organization of the colonial military units. First of all, continuing a trend that had already started during Napoleon III's reign, France's colonial troops came to include an increasingly larger number of locally-raised corps made up of natives from the various overseas territories. These had officers and NCOs provided by the naval infantry regiments and soon became a fundamental component of the Third Republic's military forces. Secondly, during the last decades of the century, France conquered several new colonies in various areas of the world and this led to a rapid expansion of the *Troupes Coloniales*. On 27 July 1872 a new conscription law was introduced for the metropolitan army, which was also applied – for

NCO of the Naval Infantry in the 1890s, wearing M1895 single-breasted campaign jacket instead of the "paletot".

Soldiers of the Naval Infantry in the 1890s; the figure on the left has the M1895 single-breasted campaign jacket, the figure on the right has the M1886 "paletot".

the first time – to the colonial troops of the navy. As a result, both the naval infantry and the naval artillery corps started to include a large number of conscripts. Thanks to the larger pool of recruits that became available, the overall number of companies included in the four regiments of naval infantry was progressively expanded to 116. By 1889, however, it became apparent that the four existing regiments had too many battalions and companies each (a single regiment, for example, had an impressive total of 45 companies). As a result, it was decided to double the number of naval infantry regiments from four to eight. Each of the existing units divided its companies in two parts in order to form a new regiment. In this way the 1st Regiment gave birth to the new 5th Regiment, the 2nd Regiment to the new 6th Regiment, the 3rd Regiment to the new 7th Regiment and the 4th Regiment to the new 8th Regiment. From 1880 the internal composition of each naval infantry company became as follows: three officers, eight senior NCOs, 10 corporals and 76 privates. Also in 1880 the single remaining battalion of naval infantry serving on the warships of the fleet – the second one had already been disbanded – was absorbed into the navy and ceased to be part of the colonial troops.

The eight naval infantry regiments existing in 1889 were always stationed in France during the period 1890–1914 and thus acted as a sort of "reserve" that could be employed overseas in case of need. For this reason, from 1890, the garrison duties in the colonies started to be performed – almost entirely – by the locally-raised units of natives having French officers and NCOs. When needed, however, temporary "ad hoc" units – known as "*régiments/bataillons de marche*" or "marching regiments/battalions" – could be formed in metropolitan France for service overseas by assembling together mixed battalions or companies coming from the various branches of the French military forces (metropolitan army, Army of Africa and Colonial Army). From 1890 some of such temporary units started to be transformed into permanent regiments of naval infantry, which were garrisoned overseas. Four new regiments of naval infantry, numbered 9–12, were created with this system. In 1888 the French colonial forces already included four "marching" units that had been transformed into permanent corps: the 1st Marching Regiment of Annam (central Vietnam), the 2nd Marching Regiment of Tonkin (northern Vietnam), the 3rd Marching Regiment of Cochinchina (southern Vietnam) and the Marching Battalion of New Caledonia. In 1889–1890 these were transformed into new permanent naval infantry regiments as follows: the 2nd Marching Regiment became the 9th Naval Infantry Regiment, the 1st Marching Regiment became the 10th Naval Infantry Regiment, the 3rd Marching Regiment became the 11th Naval Infantry Regiment and the Marching Battalion of New Caledonia became the 12th Naval Infantry Regiment. The latter unit ceased to be a regiment in January 1901, when it was transformed into the independent Colonial Battalion of New Caledonia. In 1903 a new 12th Naval Infantry Regiment was formed, but in 1907 this was disbanded and its personnel were divided between three of the other regiments. Finally, in 1907, a new 12th Naval Infantry Regiment was raised. This was quite short-lived, however, since it was disbanded and incorporated into the 11th Naval Infantry Regiment during 1912.

The expansion of the French naval infantry continued during the period 1890–1915, with the formation of several new regiments. The 13th Naval Infantry Regiment was created in January 1895 by assembling together different detachments serving in Madagascar; in 1912 it became an independent battalion with the new denomination of "*Bataillon de l'Emyrne*". The 14th Naval Infantry Regiment was formed in January 1899 by assembling together different detachments serving in Senegal; in 1903 it became an independent battalion with the new denomination of "*Bataillon de l'Afrique Occidentale Française*". The 15th Naval Infantry Regiment was created in March 1900 and served in Madagascar until being absorbed into the 13th Naval Infantry Regiment in September 1903. The 16th Naval Infantry Regiment was formed in June 1900 by converting a "marching regiment" that had been fighting in China. The 17th Naval Infantry Regiment was created in June 1900 by assembling together some "marching battalions" that had been fighting in China; it was disbanded in 1901. The 18th Naval Infantry Regiment was formed in July 1900 by assembling together some "marching battalions" that had been fighting in China; in 1907 it was transformed into the new 12th Naval Infantry Regiment that was disbanded in 1912. The last years of the 19th century saw the formation of two new regiments known as "Naval Garrison Regiments". According to the original plans, four of the latter had to be created and be employed as garrison units in the major colonies. In the end, however, only two such regiments were formed and these had a short life. In January 1901, in fact, they were transformed into the new 21st Naval Infantry Regiment and 22nd Naval Infantry Regiment (the naval infantry regiments numbered 19–20 were never created). The 23rd Naval Infantry Regiment and the 24th Naval Infantry Regiment were added to the existing ones during 1902. As a result of the complex organizational changes described above, by the outbreak of the Great War in 1914 the French Colonial Army comprised a total of 16 naval infantry regiments. From 7 July 1900 all the Naval Infantry Regiments received the new denomination of "Colonial Infantry Regiments".

In addition to the regiments described above, during the period 1889–1914 there were also several independent naval infantry corps of smaller size: the "*Bataillon de l'Afrique Occidentale Française*" created in 1903 and stationed in Senegal; the "*Bataillon des Antilles et de la Guyane*" created in 1903 and stationed in the French Caribbean colonies; the "*Bataillon de La Réunion*" created in 1901 and disbanded in 1913; the "*Bataillon de Diego-Suarez*" created in 1905 and stationed in Madagascar; the "*Bataillon de l'Emyrne*" created in 1912 and stationed in Madagascar; the "*Bataillon de Calédonie et de Tahiti*" formed in 1903 from the Colonial Battalion of New Caledonia and stationed in the Pacific. During 1912, following the French occupation of Morocco, six mixed-race regiments of colonial infantry were formed in the latter country. Each of these, known as "*Bataillons du Maroc*", consisted of one "white" colonial infantry battalion and two "black" battalions of Senegalese Tirailleurs. In 1914 the six regiments were disbanded and their best elements were consolidated to form a single "Colonial Regiment of Morocco" that participated in the Great War. The colonial troops raised in metropolitan France also comprised the "*Compagnie de Discipline de la Marine*" and the "*Corps des Disciplinaires des Colonies*". Both were penal military units made up of convicted soldiers, but the first consisted of men coming from the naval infantry regiments while the second consisted of men coming from the metropolitan army units serving overseas. The "*Compagnie de Discipline de la Marine*" was a single company and acted as the garrison of Saint-Pierre-et-Miquelon until 1873 when it was first transferred to Guadeloupe and then to Martinique. The "*Corps des Disciplinaires des Colonies*" consisted of one company in Senegal and one company in Martinique, to which a third company in Madagascar was added in 1885. During 1891 the three companies were merged together and were stationed at Diego Suarez in Madagascar.

For the Naval Artillery Regiment after the war of 1870–1871 with Prussia, it continued to consist of 28 companies deployed as follows: 11 at Lorient, 5 at Toulon, 1 at Cherbourg, 1 at Brest, 1 at Rochefort, 1 in Martinique, 1 in Guadeloupe, 1 in La Réunion, 1 in Guyana, 1 in Senegal, 1 in Tahiti, 1 in New Caledonia and 2 in Cochinchina. In September 1880 an independent company of artillery workers was organized in Senegal. During 1889 the number of naval artillery companies was increased from 28 to 34, of which 20 served in metropolitan France and 14 in the colonies. On 8 July 1893 the French Naval Artillery was re-structured in two regiments and started to also comprise some companies of mounted and mountain artillery. The new 1st Regiment of Naval Artillery included 8 foot companies, 3 mounted companies and 3 mountain companies; the new 2nd Regiment of Naval Artillery included 5 foot companies, 3 mounted companies and 1 mountain company. The 23 companies of naval artillery were grouped, for operational purposes, into two "tactical groups", one for the Asian and Pacific colonies, the other for the African and Caribbean colonies.

Uniforms and weapons

The Hohenlohe Regiment wore the standard uniform of the French line infantry that had been introduced during the Napoleonic Period with the dress regulations of 1812, but in a distinctive light blue colour. Its dress consisted of the following elements: black shako with brass front plate and white cockade, yellow top band, brass chinscale and pompom in company colour (yellow for fusilier companies, red for the grenadier company and green for the chasseur company); light blue coat with yellow frontal plastron, collar, round cuffs, cuff flaps and short turnbacks; white trousers and black gaiters. The grenadiers of the regiment had red fringed epaulettes on the shoulders, while the chasseurs had green fringed epaulettes. The early Battalions of the Colonies organized in 1815 were uniformed as follows: black shako with brass front plate and white cockade, black top band, brass chinscale and pompom in company colour (yellow for fusilier companies, red for the grenadier company and green for the chasseur company); dark blue coat with yellow piping to the frontal plastron and cuff flaps; yellow collar, round cuffs and short turnbacks; white trousers and black gaiters. The grenadiers had red fringed epaulettes on the shoulders, while the chasseurs had green fringed epaulettes. After the second restoration of the Bourbons the uniform described above was slightly changed and became as follows: black shako with brass front plate and white cockade, black top band, brass chinscale and pompom in company colour (yellow for fusilier companies, red for the grenadier company and green for the chasseur company); dark blue single-breasted coat with yellow piping to the front; dark blue collar, round cuffs, cuff flaps and shoulder straps all having yellow piping; yellow short turnbacks; white trousers and white spats. The grenadiers had red fringed epaulettes instead of the shoulder straps, while the chasseurs had green fringed epaulettes.

The Colonial Battalions, as during the Napoleonic Period, were given a distinctive iron grey uniform consisting of the following elements: black shako with brass front plate and white cockade, black top band, brass chinscale and black pompom bearing a yellow flaming grenade; iron grey coat with dark blue collar, frontal plastron and round cuffs piped in white; iron grey shoulder straps and cuffs flaps piped in dark blue; dark blue short turnbacks; iron grey trousers and black gaiters. The Naval Artillery was given the following uniform in 1815, which was practically identical to that of the army's foot artillery except for the headgear: black bearskin with red cords and flounders; dark blue coat with red collar, fringed epaulettes, cuff flaps and short turnbacks; dark blue frontal plastron and round cuffs piped in red; dark blue trousers and black gaiters. The new uniform assigned to the Naval Artillery in 1822 was identical to that of the foot artillery, except for the peculiar badge that was stamped on its buttons (an anchor placed under two crossed cannons). It consisted of the following elements: black shako with brass front plate and white cockade, red top band, brass chinscale and red pompom surmounted by a tuft of the same colour; dark blue coat with collar, frontal plastron and cuff flaps of the same colour piped in red; red fringed epaulettes, round cuffs and short turnbacks; dark blue trousers and white gaiters. The uniform given to the Naval Infantry in 1822 was identical to that of the line infantry,

Gunner of the Naval Artillery wearing M1886 khaki-brown campaign uniform.

except for the peculiar badge that was stamped on its buttons (an anchor placed under the unit's number). It consisted of the following elements: black shako with brass front plate and white cockade, brass chinscale; red top band, pompom in company colour (medium blue for fusilier companies, red for the grenadier company and yellow for the light infantry company); dark blue single-breasted coat with red collar, round cuffs and short turnbacks; red piping to the front and to the dark blue cuff flaps; dark blue shoulder straps piped in red; white trousers and white spats. The grenadiers had red fringed epaulettes instead of the shoulder straps and a red tuft over the pompom, while the light infantrymen had yellow fringed epaulettes and a yellow tuft.

With the general reorganization of 1831 the uniform of the Naval Infantry did not change, while that of the Naval Artillery became as follows: black shako with brass front plate and white cockade having red lace holder, red top band, brass chinscale, red top band and red pompom surmounted by a falling plume of the same colour, red inverted chevrons on each side; dark blue coat with collar and frontal plastron piped in red; red fringed epaulettes, pointed cuffs and short turnbacks; white trousers and white gaiters. In 1843 the dress described above was slightly changed, with the addition of red cords and flounders to the shako and with the introduction of new dark blue trousers having double red side-stripe. The new dress regulations promulgated in 1845 for the Naval Infantry caused a real revolution in the uniforms of France's colonial troops, since they introduced a new garment that soon became iconic and distinctive of the Naval Infantry: the "*paletot*". This was a double-breasted tunic of naval cut, which could be left partly unbuttoned on the front. The M1845 dress of the Naval Infantry was as follows: black shako with brass front plate and chinscale, red top band and chevrons on each side, white cockade (tricolour since 1848), pompom in the distinctive colour of each regiment for the centre companies and in yellow for the elite ones; dark blue double-breasted and long-skirted "*paletot*" tunic, with red piping to the front, folded collar and pointed cuffs; red anchor badge embroidered on each side of the collar; dark blue shoulder straps with red fringed epaulettes for the centre companies and yellow fringed epaulettes for the elite companies; the first three buttons of the tunic were left unbuttoned to show a white shirt and a black tie (another two elements that became peculiar to the Naval Infantry's uniform); white trousers and white spats. In 1852 Napoleon III promulgated new dress regulations for both the Naval Infantry and the Naval Artillery. The uniform of the Naval Infantry became as follows: black shako with brass front plate and chinscale, red top band and chevrons on each side, tricolour cockade and yellow pompom surmounted by a tuft of the same colour; dark blue double-breasted tunic (resembling the original "*paletot*" in shape) with red piping to the front, standing collar and pointed cuffs; red anchor badge embroidered on each side of the collar; yellow fringed epaulettes; light blue trousers with red side-stripe and black spats. The M1852 uniform of the Naval Artillery was not very different from the previous one, except for the new forward-pointing shako. It consisted of the following elements: black shako with brass front plate and tricolour cockade having red lace holder, red top band, brass chinscale, red cords and flounders and red pompom surmounted by a falling plume of the same colour, red chevrons on each side; dark blue tunic with collar, frontal plastron and pointed cuffs piped in red; red fringed epaulettes and short turnbacks; dark blue trousers with double red side-stripe and white gaiters.

After the fall of Napoleon III's "Second Empire", in 1873, the following parade dress was adopted by the French Naval Infantry (which remained practically unchanged until 1914): dark blue képi with red quarter-piping and brass badge on the front; dark blue double-breasted short tunic with red piping to standing collar, front and round cuffs; red anchor badge embroidered on each side of the collar; yellow fringed epaulettes, dark blue trousers with red side-stripe. Campaign dress – formalized in 1886 – consisted of a white tropical helmet made of cork and of a dark blue "*paletot*" without any piping that had a red anchor badge embroidered on each side of the collar. The campaign outfit was completed by white cotton trousers and white spats. In 1895 a new single-breasted dark blue jacket was introduced for campaign use; this had red collar patches bearing a dark blue anchor badge and dark blue shoulder straps. Until 1883 the officers of the Naval Infantry were dressed like their men, except for having gold piping; in that year they were given a black single-breasted patrol jacket with black braiding on the external edges and black frogging on the front. Rank was shown by golden "Hungarian knots" embroidered on the sleeves. In 1893 the officers of the Naval Infantry were given a new dark blue single-breasted short tunic having gold shoulder bars and gold rank rings around the cuffs. From 1886, for campaign use overseas, the French Naval Infantry was given a collarless single-breasted jacket of a brownish khaki colour; this had shoulder straps and two side-pockets in addition to dark blue collar patches bearing a red anchor. With the introduction of the new uniform, khaki trousers and khaki covers for the tropical helmet came into use. In 1895 the Naval Infantry was also given an entirely white tropical uniform, comprising a single-breasted jacket with standing collar and shoulder straps. Like the khaki jacket this one also had side-pockets and dark blue collar patches bearing a red anchor. In 1901 a new version of the khaki campaign dress was introduced, having a lighter colour and flapped skirt pockets.

For the Naval Artillery, in 1872 it was given the following parade uniform: dark blue képi with red quarter-piping and brass badge on the front; dark blue double-breasted short tunic with red standing collar and pointed cuffs, yellow flaming grenade badge embroidered on the collar, red "contre-epaulettes" and black frontal frogging with three rows of buttons; dark blue trousers with a single red stripe placed between two larger stripes of the same colour. On campaign the képi was replaced with the white tropical helmet and the tunic with a dark blue single-breasted jacket having collar patches bearing a yellow badge (consisting of a flaming grenade placed above an anchor). The uniforms of the officers followed the same evolution of those worn by the Naval Infantry's officers. Also the Naval Artillery used the M1886 and M1901 khaki dress as well as the M1895 white tropical uniform. The "*Compagnies de Discipline de la Marine*" and the "*Corps des Disciplinaires des Colonies*" were dressed like the Naval Infantry but entirely in iron grey instead of dark blue. During the whole period 1815–1914 the French Naval and Colonial troops always employed the same equipment and weapons of the metropolitan military forces, which have already been described in the previous chapters dedicated to the Army of Africa.

The Native Troops, 1815–1914

Africa

Senegal and French Sudan

The French colonization of Senegal began in 1659, when the first commercial outpost of Saint-Louis was founded by some French merchants on the coastline of the African country. From 1664 the small coastal colony came under the control of the French government. In 1677 some French warships conquered the strategic island of Gorée, located off Senegal's coast, from the Dutch settlers who had already colonized it. By the end of the 17th century the French presence in Senegal was already well established and Gorée had become the main logistic centre of the French slave trade. In 1758, during the Seven Years' War, the British attacked Senegal and conquered it from the French; the latter, however, retook their colony during 1779 as part of their country's participation in the American Revolution. During the Revolutionary Wars Senegal was menaced and attacked several times by British military forces and in 1809 the French colony was finally occupied by Great Britain. However it was returned to the Bourbons by the Congress of Vienna. The various French governments that were in place during the period 1815–1852 showed very little interest in Senegal, largely because after the independence of Haiti in 1803 the French slave trade ceased to be a flourishing activity. This situation changed only with the ascendancy of Napoleon III who, in 1854, structured Gorée and the French outposts in continental Senegal as two distinct colonies. This administrative subdivision, however, did not last for long since in 1859 Gorée was re-united with the rest of Senegal in order to form a single colony. Until 1845 the colony of Senegal did not have any locally-raised unit, since its garrison was provided by the naval/colonial corps described in the previous chapter. During the early 1840s, however, the French authorities in Senegal started to feel the need for some mounted soldiers who could patrol the vast Senegalese countryside more rapidly than the infantry forces placed under their command. The interior areas of Senegal were inhabited by tribal communities having great horsemanship traditions and these could field sizeable contingents of mounted warriors. As a result, the French absolutely needed to deploy a well-equipped cavalry unit in their colony of Western Africa. On 21 July 1845 one corps of the Army of Africa, the 6th Squadron of the 1st Regiment of Spahis, was detached from its parent unit and was sent to Senegal in order to become part of the local military garrison. The Algerian Spahis allocated to serve in Senegal, 120 men in total, arrived in Dakar (the main centre of the colony) during the early months of 1847. During the following years the cavalry unit continued to consist of Algerians, but with of time an increasing number of Senegalese recruits started to be included in the ranks of the corps. These soon proved to be excellent cavalry soldiers, especially after their squadron was deployed against the rebel tribes of the interior. In May 1853 the number of soldiers in the unit was increased to 186; by that time the original Alge-

Trooper of the Senegalese Spahis with M1858 dress, including tropical helmet made of cork.

rian troopers had been replaced by new Senegalese ones but the squadron – which official denomination was "Squadron of Senegalese Spahis" – still comprised a strong French cadre of 43 troopers in addition to the French officers and NCOs of the original Algerian unit. By 1856 the squadron had been greatly expanded and comprised 250 men. During the following decades the Senegalese Spahis earned an excellent military reputation by participating in all the colonial expeditions conducted by the French in Western Africa and Equatorial Africa. They played a prominent role in the little-known military campaigns that finally connected Algeria with Senegal across the Sahara. From their depot of Saint-Louis the elite Squadron of Senegalese Spahis also provided experienced cadres for the formation of new locally-raised cavalry units across French Western Africa and Equatorial Africa. These temporary corps, existing during 1897–1904, were collectively known as "Auxiliary Spahis". They were made up of tribesmen enlisted as semi-regular soldiers to perform a specific duty (like guarding a tract of frontier) or to fight in a single campaign. Their members either wore no uniforms or a simplified version of the Senegalese Spahis' dress. On 29 August 1893 a new squadron of native cavalry was raised from the tribesmen of French Sudan, a territory roughly corresponding to present-day Mali. This was soon followed by a second squadron, which was disbanded in 1897. The "Squadron of Sudanese Spahis" formed in 1893 was merged with the Senegalese Spahis on 15 August 1902. As a result, the latter corps started to comprise the 1st Squadron of Senegalese Spahis (recruited from Senegal) and the 2nd Squadron of Senegalese Spahis (recruited from French Sudan).

During the early decades of their presence in Senegal the French never formed a locally-raised infantry unit, since they did not consider the locals particularly reliable for military service. This changed after the ascendancy of Napoleon III, who was strongly determined to enlarge the French settlement in Western Africa in order to connect it with the French possessions in Algeria. In April 1852 the Emperor authorized the formation of two infantry companies made up of native soldiers in Senegal. These would serve as garrison troops and be commanded/trained by French officers. The creation of these two companies was a sort of "experiment", since at that time – not counting the Army of Africa – the French colonial troops included just two small units of native soldiers (the Cipahis in India and the Black Chasseurs in Guyana). The main reason behind the formation of the two Senegalese companies was the fact that most of the colonial soldiers coming from metropolitan France did not like serving in Senegal, since the natural environment of the latter territory was particularly inhospitable for white individuals. One of the new companies was garrisoned at Dakar, the other on the island of Gorée. After some years it became apparent that the experiment had worked well, since the Senegalese native soldiers performed their duties with excellent discipline. As a result, on 21 July 1857, the two companies were transformed into a permanent battalion of the French colonial military forces and received the official denomination of "Senegalese Tirailleurs". The new battalion was to consist of six companies with 86 men each, natives who volunteered to serve under the French flag or ex-slaves who were purchased and freed by the French government. The corps, at least initially, also included a certain number of former prisoners of war who had been captured by the French and who had decided to join the latter's cause. The officers of the corps were all French, while the NCOs were mostly chosen from former native war chieftains. Despite their official denomination, the "Senegalese Tirailleurs" did not only consist of soldiers coming from present-day Senegal, since they were also recruited from warlike tribes living in southern Niger. Initially the French colonial authorities had planned to employ the

Trooper of the Senegalese Spahis with M1879 dress.

Above, left: NCO of the Senegalese Spahis with M1879 uniform; on parade the tall red "fez" was worn instead of the tropical helmet. ASKB

Above, right: Trooper of the Senegalese Spahis with the white summer version of the M1879 dress.

Left: Native officer of the Senegalese Tirailleurs with M1857 dress.

Right: Private of the Senegalese Tirailleurs with M1857 dress.

NCO of the Senegalese Tirailleurs with M1868 campaign uniform.

Private of the Senegalese Tirailleurs with M1889 dress.

NCO of the Senegalese Tirailleurs with M1889 dress, photographed in the early years of the 20th century.

Senegalese Tirailleurs only as a sort of militarized constabulary, but with the progression of time it became apparent that these African soldiers were excellent fighters. They were courageous in battle, could live with very little food for very long periods, could travel long distances on harsh terrain and were extremely loyal to their officers. Like the Senegalese Spahis, the Senegalese Tirailleurs participated in all the military campaigns fought by France in Western Africa and Equatorial Africa, always remaining the most reliable locally-raised corps of the French colonial forces. As we will see, they also provided experienced cadres for the formation of new native infantry units across French Western Africa and Equatorial Africa. In 1882 the number of men in each company of the battalion was increased from 86 to 120. By that time the Senegalese Tirailleurs also had a small autonomous detachment garrisoned in the new French colony of Gabon (this detachment existed until 1887). On 31 August 1884, as a result of their success, the Senegalese Tirailleurs were transformed into a regiment with eight companies. Five years later the number of companies was increased to ten and these were grouped into two battalions that remained part of a single regiment. On 26 August 1890 the Regiment of Senegalese Tirailleurs saw a further expansion, since a third battalion was added to its establishment. During 1893–1894, for the duration of the campaign that led to the French occupation of Dahomey, the various companies of Senegalese Tirailleurs mobilized for the expedition were temporarily grouped into a "marching regiment". As with the Senegalese Spahis, the French colonial authorities expanded their Senegalese Tirailleurs by forming some new locally-raised units in the region of French Sudan (present-day Mali). On 23 April 1892 two battalions with four companies each were recruited from the warlike inhabitants of French Sudan and were grouped together as the Regiment of Sudanese Tirailleurs. This, like that of the Senegalese Tirailleurs, proved to be an excellent corps and thus was expanded quite rapidly. A third battalion was added to its establishment on 9 August 1893, followed by a fourth one on 7 March 1894. The Sudanese Tirailleurs participated in several military campaigns during the last years of the 19th century, playing a prominent role in the process that culminated with the French colonization of Western Sahara. On 7 May 1900 the French government decided to absorb the Sudanese Tirailleurs into the Senegalese Tirailleurs; the latter, as a result, were reorganized on two regiments: the 1st Regiment of Senegalese Tirailleurs and the 2nd Regiment of Senegalese Tirailleurs (former Sudanese Tirailleurs). The new 2nd Regiment was re-structured in two battalions, raised to three in 1906.

Private of the Sudanese Tirailleurs.

NCO of the Sudanese Tirailleurs (left) and private of the Congolese Tirailleurs (right).

During 1900, by converting a temporary unit recruited from Western African soldiers who were serving in Madagascar, the 3rd Regiment of Senegalese Tirailleurs was formed. This, however, was quite short-lived since it was disbanded on 1 February 1911 in order to provide the cadres for a new locally-raised unit of natives in Madagascar (the 4th Regiment of Malagasy Tirailleurs). In 1908 a single platoon of "*méharistes*" mounted on dromedaries, consisting of 2 French NCOs and 117 Sudanese rankers, was added to the 2nd Regiment of Senegalese Tirailleurs. This detachment was mostly tasked with patrolling the southern areas of French Sahara. A 4th Regiment of Senegalese Tirailleurs was organized in 1904 by assembling together several detachments of Senegalese Tirailleurs that were serving in the Ivory Coast and in Dahomey (modern Benin). Temporarily disbanded in 1906, this was re-raised during 1907. A new 3rd Regiment of Senegalese Tirailleurs was formed in 1912 and – like the existing three – served with distinction during the Great War. During 1912, following the French occupation of Morocco, six mixed-race regiments of colonial infantry were formed in the latter country. Each of these, known as "*Bataillons du Maroc*", consisted of one "white" colonial infantry battalion and two "black" battalions of Senegalese Tirailleurs. In 1914 the six regiments were disbanded and their best elements were consolidated to form a single "Colonial Regiment of Morocco" that participated in the Great War. In addition to the more famous Senegalese Spahis and Senegalese Tirailleurs, the French colonial authorities in Senegal could also count on a squadron of locally-raised mounted gendarmerie known as "Native Gendarmes of Senegal". This unit of armed constabulary was organized in 1894 and took over most of the police duties from the Spahis. The French colonial authorities also raised some units of auxiliary artillery drivers from both Senegal and French Sudan. A first company of artillery drivers – attached to the Naval Artillery – was created in Senegal during 1881. By 1914 this had been joined by another two companies of the same kind. In 1884 an independent company of artillery drivers, not attached to the Naval Artillery, was also raised in Senegal. A single company of artillery drivers from French Sudan, attached to the Naval Artillery, was created in 1892.

Ivory Coast, Benin, Gabon and Guinea

With the progression of time, France created several new colonies in Western Africa and Equatorial Africa. Each of these, of course, raised its own colonial military units made up of natives. On 29 June 1891 an infantry battalion was raised from the Hausa tribes; the latter were particularly warlike and lived over a vast area of Western Africa that comprised southern Tchad, southern Niger, Gabon and the Ivory Coast. This "Battalion of Hausa Tirailleurs" fought with distinction during the French conquest of Dahomey but was disbanded in 1897. In March 1895, for service in Madagascar, a new "Marching Battalion of Hausa Tirailleurs" was raised. This continued to exist until 1900, when it was disbanded to form the new 3rd Regiment of Senegalese Tirailleurs that existed until 1911. On 9 November 1889 the French colonial authorities of Dahomey (present-day southern Benin) raised a single company of native armed constabulary known as "Native Civil Guard of Dahomey". This, over time, was expanded to reach an establishment of three companies (each having 3 French officers and 115 native policemen). The Native Civil Guard of Dahomey was mostly tasked with crushing tribal revolts and performed quite well on several occasions. By 1914 it had been enlarged and re-structured in 15 platoon-sized "brigades" that could deploy around 500 men. During the early years of the 20th century a similar police corps, known as "Native Civil Guard of the Ivory Coast", was organized by the French in the latter country. Until 1887, as anticipated in the previous paragraph, the French colony of Gabon was garrisoned by a small detachment provided by the Senegalese Tirailleurs. In that year, after the Senegalese soldiers went back to Dakar, two locally-raised infantry companies of Gabonese natives were formed. These, known as "Gabonese Tirailleurs", became a permanent corps on 25 August 1889 and continued to comprise cadres provided by the Senegalese Tirailleurs for several years. After having been reduced to a single company, the Gabonese Tirailleurs were disbanded in 1891. On 1st January 1912 they were re-formed, with cadres mostly recruited in Senegal, as the "Gabonese Regiment of Senegalese Tirailleurs" with two battalions. The colony of Guinea formed its first native corps in 1907, when a single infantry battalion known as "Battalion of Guinea" was created. This was later transformed into the independent 4th Battalion of Senegalese Tirailleurs.

Private of the Hausa Tirailleurs.

Congo

In 1902, following their expansion in Equatorial Africa, the French raised a new native infantry battalion in what later became French Congo. This, known as "Native Battalion of Congo", had cadres provided by the Senegalese Tirailleurs. Just one month after its organization, on 6 October 1902, the battalion saw its companies being increased from four to eight and thus the corps received the new denomination of "Native Infantry Regiment of Congo". In 1903 the name of the unit became "Congolese Regiment of Senegalese Tirailleurs". The latter was the largest military unit deployed by France in Equatorial Africa and most of its companies were garrisoned at Brazzaville.

Tchad, Mauritania, Niger and Mali

In 1900, following their expansion in Western Africa, the French formed two new battalions of native infantry in Tchad with cadres taken from the Senegalese Tirailleurs. The two new corps were the "Native Battalion of Chari" with three companies and the "Mixed Battalion of Tchad" with five companies. According to the original plans of the French authorities, the Senegalese members of the two units would be replaced with native volunteers progressively recruited in Tchad, but this happened only at a very slow pace. Attached to each of the two battalions there were an auxiliary squadron of local cavalry and a small section of artillery. In 1910 the two corps were assembled together in order to form the new "Tchadian Regiment of Senegalese Tirailleurs". As is clear from the latter denomination, the native units raised from Senegalese cadres retained the adjective "Senegalese" in their title after most of their members started to be recruited from other colonies of French Western or Equatorial Africa. From 1902 the French colonial authorities of Mauritania, Niger and Mali started to raise some native troops in the territories under their control. The first of such units to be formed was the so-called "Battalion of Zinder", raised during 1902 in Niger; the second was the "Battalion of Timbuktu" that was created during 1907 in Mali; the third was the "Battalion of

Mauritania" that was formed during 1908 in Mauritania. These three battalions had a quite "static" nature and were mostly tasked with patrolling the borders of their respective colonies. For this reason they were collectively known as "Territorial Battalions of Tirailleurs". In 1910 the French authorities decided to reorganize the three units as independent "Battalions of Senegalese Tirailleurs", numbered 1–3. The adjective "Senegalese" of the new denomination did not reflect the ethnic composition of the battalions' members but was due to the fact that these three units were formed from Senegalese cadres. As a result of the new organization the Battalion of Mauritania became the 1st Battalion of Senegalese Tirailleurs, the Battalion of Zinder became the 2nd Battalion of Senegalese Tirailleurs and the Battalion of Timbuktu became the 3rd Battalion of Senegalese Tirailleurs. As we have seen in one of the previous paragraphs, a 4th Battalion of Senegalese Tirailleurs was formed in the colony of Gabon. In addition to the infantry units listed above, the colonies of Tchad, Mauritania, Niger and Mali also had some small corps of "*méharistes*" (i.e. soldiers mounted on dromedaries and employed for patrolling desert areas). In 1901 a platoon of "*méharistes*" was organized at Zinder in Niger, followed by a second one at Kanem in Tchad during 1903 and by a third one at Boutilimit in Mauritania during 1905. By 1907 the "*méharistes*" of French Western Africa and Equatorial Africa had been expanded and comprised the following units: three sections in Mauritania, four sections in Mali, three sections in Niger and one company in Tchad. During 1908 the "*méharistes*" were re-organized again and came to comprise the following corps: three platoons in Mauritania, four platoons in Mali, four platoons in Niger, one company and one platoon in Tchad.

French Somaliland

During the last decades of the 19th century the coast of Somaliland, in Eastern Africa, was controlled by aggressive bands of pirates who attacked the European merchant ships that passed across the Red Sea. Following some incidents that involved French ships, in 1896 France decided to occupy the main port of central Somaliland, the city of Djibouti, in order to transform it from a base of pirates to a new colony. The latter, despite being very small, started to play an important role inside the French colonial empire due to its strategic location. Being isolated from the rest of France's colonies, the garrison of French Somaliland was always quite small and depended, from an administrative point of view, on the French colonial forces in Madagascar. Initially it consisted of a small detachment of Senegalese Tirailleurs plus some local irregular auxiliaries. In 1910 the French authorities decided to raise a native constabulary corps, known as "Native Guard Brigade of Somaliland", consisting of a single company with 200 men. Some small squads of policemen mounted on dromedaries were later added to the corps, in order to patrol the interior areas of the colony.

Madagascar:

During the second half of the 18th century both France and Great Britain started to have an increasing interest in Madagascar, the largest island of the African continent, located in the Indian Ocean. The strategic geographical position of Madagascar made it very important for international commerce, since it was located half-way between the rich coastal centres of Eastern Africa and the newly-created European colonial outposts in India. Both France and Great Britain developed plans for the colonization of the large island, but the French were advantaged by the fact that they already had two colonies located not

Private of the Sakalava Tirailleurs.

far from Madagascar (Isle-de-Bourbon and Isle-de-France). In 1817, after centuries of inter-tribal warfare that ravaged most of the island, Madagascar was unified as a single kingdom by the Merina people. The latter inhabited in the northern part of Madagascar and were particularly warlike. The Merina kings and queens who ruled over the large island did of their best to transform their realm into a strong centralized monarchy, which could preserve its independence under the increasing pressure exerted by the colonial powers. The British, after the unification of Madagascar, preferred to recognize the legitimacy of the Merina Kingdom instead of attempting a military occupation of the island. As a result, from the 1820s Great Britain became the main international ally of the Merina Kingdom and started to provide military instructors to the latter. The various monarchs of Madagascar, in fact, gradually "modernized" their military forces by equipping them with surplus flintlock muskets purchased from Great Britain and by having them trained in the European way. Radama I, the monarch who unified Madagascar, considered the French as his worst enemies and thus on several occasions he insulted the French authorities and merchants who visited his kingdom. In 1829, in order to punish Radama I for his hostile attitude, the French organized a punitive expedition against Madagascar. This reached Tamatave Bay and saw the French occupation of Tintingue. After the French vessels bombarded the city of Tamatave, the hostilities progressively came to an end because of the outbreak of the 1830 Revolution in metropolitan France. The expedition of 1829 led to the occupation of some outposts on the coastline of Madagascar, but these were all progressively abandoned by the French who did not have any remaining base on the island by 1833.

In 1855 the heir to the throne of Madagascar and future king, Radama II, granted numerous lucrative economic privileges to a French merchant named Joseph-François Lambert. The latter had been enough intelligent to become a member of the Merina court and to start exerting an increasing influence over the young Radama II. In 1861 the latter became king but ruled for just two years, since he was assassinated in 1863. The death of Radama II was a major blow for the French colonial ambitions in Madagascar, since in 1863 the new Merina government revoked all the concessions that had been made to Lambert. British influence became increasingly stronger in Madagascar over time, since the Merina Kingdom was modernized under the guidance of British individuals. In 1877 slavery was abolished in Madagascar and in 1879 a new conscription law was introduced by the British instructors who were training the Merina military forces. The legal system was reformed in 1878 and a new constitution was promulgated in 1881. Around 1880 the French started to fear – correctly – that Madagascar could become a British protectorate and thus decided to attack the Merina Kingdom. They could count on the support of the Sakalava minority living in eastern Madagascar, which had remained faithful to the short-lived protectorate established over their lands by the French in 1829. The killing of a French citizen in Madagascar's capital of Tananarivo was the "casus belli" that finally led to the first French invasion of the Merina Kingdom. The latter is commonly known as "First Franco-Hova War", since the term "Hova" was at that time employed to designate the free commoners of the Merina Kingdom. The society of Madagascar, in fact, comprised three principal castes: the Andriana (nobles), the Hova (free commoners) and the Andevo (slaves). The hostilities of the First Franco-Hova War began in May 1883, when the French fleet blockaded Madagascar's coastline and bombarded several coastal settlements. On 17 May the French occupied Majunga and then continued their naval bombardments. During the early months of 1885 the French colonial forces occupied Diego-Suarez Bay, but the resistance mounted by the Hova soldiers and by their British instructors proved to be very strong. During those same months France became involved in a war with China for possession of northern Vietnam and thus no major reinforcements could be sent to Madagascar. As a result of this and of the great logistical difficulties encountered by the French troops operating in Madagascar, the French government decided to end the hostilities with the signing of a peace treaty in December 1885. According to this a large war indemnity had to be paid by the Merina Kingdom to France. The treaty, however, was never applied and this was one of the main causes behind the outbreak of the Second Franco-Hova War.

On 5 August 1890 a diplomatic agreement was signed between France and Great Britain, according to which the French

NCO of the Malagasy Tirailleurs.

recognized Zanzibar as a British protectorate and the British recognized Madagascar as a French protectorate. After signing this agreement, France had a free hand in Madagascar, as the British military instructors left the Merina Kingdom. Conquering the whole island, however, would have been a very difficult enterprise due to the harsh nature of the local terrain and to the unhealthy climate that was extremely dangerous for any European individual living in Madagascar. In October 1894, after the failure of some diplomatic negotiations, the new war between France and the Merina Kingdom began. The French assembled an impressive invasion force of 15,000 soldiers, which reached Madagascar in January 1895. They quite rapidly occupied Tamatave and disembarked at Majunga, initiating a campaign that would be extremely complex. After landing, the French troops started to experience serious problems. First of all, they suffered severe losses due to tropical diseases and had to face a chronic shortage of supplies. Madagascar had no roads at that time and thus moving large military contingents across the interior areas was extremely difficult. The French troops had to build a new road while advancing across the impenetrable jungle that covered a good portion of Madagascar. During March-April 1895 the French advanced towards Tananarivo and occupied several enemy cities, but on 6 May they had to stop in order to reorganize themselves. During June-July they had to advance on harsh mountain terrain while being constantly attacked by the Hovas, who employed hit-and-run guerrilla tactics. In August the French decided to assemble a special "task force" made up of their best troops and sent it against Tananarivo. This token force covered an impressive distance of 150 kilometres in just 16 days and finally occupied the Hova capital on 30 September. Initially the French wanted to transform Madagascar into a protectorate and thus tried to organize a new local government that could be favourable to them. This, however, proved to be impossible due to the strong anti-French feelings existing among the Hovas. As a result, on 11 December 1895, Madagascar was officially annexed to the French domains as a new colony. During the years 1896 and 1897 the French military forces were heavily involved into the "pacification" of Madagascar, in a process that saw the colonial troops committing several atrocities. Some important personalities of the former Merina Kingdom were executed in public and every form of resistance was crushed with ferocity.

When the French invaded Madagascar for the first time in 1883, the Hova Army had already been completely re-organized by its British military instructors and was one of the most effective native armies of Africa. Unlike the armed forces of all the other African states of the time, the Hova Army had a European-style structure and its members were mostly equipped with firearms. The "westernized" Hova military forces were organized from 1879, following the promulgation of a new conscription law that was inspired by the British instructors. According to this, every able-bodied Hova man aged 18 had to serve for a period of five years in the military forces of his country. At the end of this period of service, however, he could still be called to serve in case of emergencies like a foreign invasion. As a result of the above, at least potentially, the Hova Army could consist of all the able-bodied adult males of Madagascar. It should be noted, however, that the Merina government rarely mobilized all the new conscripts who became available for military service every year. It was common practice for the central authorities, in fact, to determine the needed number of soldiers every year and this was largely fewer than the number of conscripts who could be potentially mobilized. The castes of the nobles and of the slaves were exempt from military service, so as a result all the soldiers were Hovas. The operations of recruitment were carried on by the provincial governors, who could give exemptions from military service at their will. This meant that many free commoners who could pay to corrupt their provincial governor were able to avoid compulsory military service. The latter was not particularly loved by most of the Hovas, who lived off agriculture and thus did not want to leave their fields for a period of five years. Desertion was extremely common and many young Hovas, in order to avoid military service, fled to the densely-forested areas of Madagascar where they formed large

Grenadier (left) and chasseur (right) of Isle-de-Bourbon's Militia in 1816.

bands of bandits known as "*fahavalos*". Due to the recruiting problems described above, on most occasions the provincial governors were obliged to mobilize conscripts who were too young or too old to serve in the army. They were responsible for the effective formation of the Hova military forces and thus if they failed to assemble the number of soldiers required by the central government they could be removed from their posts. The new conscripts assembled at the beginning of every new year were all transferred to the capital of Tananarivo, where they were assigned to the various military units.

In total the Hova Army had around 45,000 soldiers and every year 6,000/7,000 new recruits replaced a similar number of soldiers who had completed their period of compulsory military service. The army was organized in six "corps", each of which was provided by one of the six provinces that made up the Merina Kingdom. Each "army corps" was structured in three "brigades"; a single "brigade" was formed by three or four battalions with 700 or 800 men each. A single battalion was organized in seven or eight companies with 100 soldiers each and this was the internal composition of a standard company: one captain, one lieutenant, five sergeants and 93 privates. Each battalion had an overall commander, who was responsible for the mobilization of all the companies that were placed under his orders. As a result of the above organization, each of the six "army corps" comprised a number of soldiers that varied from a minimum of 6,300 to a maximum of 9,600. A "brigade" could have from a minimum of 2,100 to a maximum of 3,200 men. In addition to the six standard "army corps", the Hova Army also comprised an elite seventh corps that acted as the Royal Guard of the Merina monarchs. The Hova Royal Guard consisted of 4,200 soldiers organized into six battalions with 700 men each, with the battalions grouped into two "brigades". The soldiers of the Hova Royal Guard were chosen from the most loyal members of the Merina tribal groups and had the privilege of living in their houses with their families. Every week only 300 of them, according to a complex system of turns, were called to serve in the capital of Tananarivo where they garrisoned the royal buildings. The royal guardsmen, called "*marakely*", were all veteran soldiers who had already completed their period of compulsory military service and who had distinguished themselves in battle.

The soldiers of the Royal Guard, unlike the other members of the Hova Army, were still armed in a traditional way with throwing spears and round shields. The Hova Army did not include any cavalry unit but had a single battalion of artillery that had been trained by a British major. This consisted of 600 men and was equipped with 85 guns of small calibre, mostly M1875 Hotchkiss mountain guns of 42mm, as well as with 10 Gardner machine guns. The Hova infantry was armed with a total of 40,000 muskets or rifles imported from Europe. Some 9,000 of these were old Brown Bess flintlocks and 31,000 were either British M1866 Snider-Enfield or US M1867 Remington breech-loaders. In case of need, the soldiers of the Royal Guard could be equipped with Remington rifles that were preserved for them in the army's stores. In addition to the regular army (called "*Imerina*") and Royal Guard, the Hova military forces could also count on the so-called "Provincial Guard". This was a sort of para-military police that was responsible for keeping order in the provinces and thus did not have a great military value. It consisted of around 14,000 policemen, 4,000 of whom were ex-soldiers provided by the Merina tribal groups. The latter were responsible for training the other 10,000 policemen who were provided by other ethnic groups. The members of the Provincial Guard lived with their families, had no formal discipline and were mostly armed with traditional weapons. They did not have uniforms, unlike the regular soldiers of the "*Imerina*" who wore a simple standard dress consisting of the following elements: dark blue or white visorless round cap with red bottom band, dark blue or white single-breasted short tunic with red

Artilleryman (left) and cavalryman (right) of Isle-de-Bourbon's Militia in 1816.

collar and round cuffs, dark blue or white trousers. The Royal Guard had a similar uniform but with different colours: white cap with dark blue bottom band, white tunic with dark blue collar and round cuffs, dark blue trousers. All the Hova soldiers served barefoot. The civilian dress of the Provincial Guard was that worn by all the male inhabitants of Madagascar, which consisted of a tall and wide-brimmed straw hat as well as of the "*lambas*", a white piece of cloth that was worn as a sort of blouse over a white shirt.

The French formed their first locally-raised colonial unit in Madagascar several years before conquering the latter country. In 1869, in fact, they created a single company of "Sakalava Tirailleurs" on the small island of Nosy Be. The latter, located not far from Madagascar and occupied by France since 1840, was inhabited by the Sakalava ethnic group that also populated most of eastern Madagascar. The Sakalavas were at war with the Merina royal government for most of the 19th century and thus always remained loyal allies of the French from 1829. The company, initially employed only as a depot for the recruiting of new soldiers, was transformed into a permanent corps on 12 August 1885 when it received the official denomination of "Company of Sakalava Tirailleurs". After the end of the first Franco-Hova War, the corps was transferred to the island of Diego-Suarez (located along the coastline of Madagascar) that had been occupied by the French. On 30 May 1892 it was renamed as the "Tirailleurs of Diego-Suarez" and was expanded to comprise two companies of Sakalava volunteers. On 13 January 1895 the unit was disbanded and absorbed into the new "Regiment of Malagasy Tirailleurs". For the Second Franco-Hova War the French authorities created a temporary "Colonial Regiment of Madagascar" that consisted of one battalion of Hausa Tirailleurs, one battalion of white "Volunteers of La Réunion" and one "Malagasy Battalion". The latter mostly consisted of Sakalaves who were recruited by the French after the beginning of the hostilities. In June 1896, however, the corps was completely re-structured in two battalions entirely recruited from Western Africa. Four years later, in 1900, it became the new 3rd Regiment of Senegalese Tirailleurs (see one of the previous paragraphs for more details). On 13 January 1895, always by recruiting significant numbers of Sakalaves from eastern Madagascar, the French formed the "Regiment of Malagasy Tirailleurs". This consisted of three battalions and supported the French in the final phase of the Second Franco-Hova War as well as in the subsequent "pacification" of Madagascar. On 6 June 1897 the corps was expanded to comprise four battalions and received the new denomination of "1st Regiment of Malagasy Tirailleurs" since, on that same date, a "2nd Regiment of Malagasy Tirailleurs" was also formed. On 25 April 1903, following the success of the two existing units, the new 3rd Regiment of Malagasy Tirailleurs was raised. A 4th Regiment of Malagasy Tirailleurs was created in 1911 by converting the former 3rd Regiment of Senegalese Tirailleurs that had been formed in 1900 with West African soldiers who had served in Madagascar. As clear from the above, the Malagasy Tirailleurs were the only native infantry corps created by the French in Africa that always remained distinct from the Senegalese Tirailleurs. They were mostly employed on their home territory and performed their duties with distinction.

Indian Ocean, Pacific Ocean and the Caribbean

In 1815, with the first restoration of the Bourbons, the militia of Isle-de-Bourbon was completely reorganized, into a mixed-race corps comprising both French settlers and natives. The militia consisted of infantry companies as well as of cavalry and artillery ones but never became a regular military corps. The first entirely native units of La Réunion (former Isle-de-Bourbon) were raised in July 1883, when two companies of volunteers (the "*Volontaires de La Réunion*") were formed. These were made up of creoles who descended from the first French settlers of the island and who were renowned for their accurate shooting. The two companies served in Madagascar during 1883–1884 before being disbanded in 1885. In December 1894 a new corps of "*Volontaires de La Réunion*" was formed, this time consisting of three companies (later increased to four) with 200 men each. The volunteers from La Réunion fought with distinction in Madagascar during 1894–1895, before being disbanded in December 1895. The Comores Islands, located between Mozambique and Madagascar, became a French protectorate during the years 1886–1897. Despite being quite near to the African coastline, their population mostly consisted of individuals having Arabic blood. After being colonized by the French, several islands of the archipelago started to organize small militia detachments consisting of 20–25 men each and being armed with old French Chassepot rifles. The Pacific island of New Caledonia, since 1878, also had some small militia detachments of this kind that were collectively known as "*Tirailleurs Canaques*" from the name of the local population. The isolated island of Tahiti had a single company of local volunteers from 1880. This small unit, known as "*Volontaires Tahitiens*", mostly served on the Marquesas Islands. The French colonies of the Caribbean area never had locally-raised military units during the period 1815–1914, except for the "Company of Cayenne's Black Chasseurs" that existed in Guyana until 1859 (see one of the previous chapters for more details on it).

India

During the Seven Years' War, especially after the decisive Battle of Plassey in 1757, France lost most its colonial outposts in India that were then occupied by the British. One important coastal city, however, remained under French control after 1763 in spite of Great Britain's ascendancy as the leading colonial power of the Indian sub-continent: the large urban centre of Pondichéry. The latter remained French until 1954 and thus was commonly known as "French India" during the historical period covered in the present book. As with their British rivals, the French began recruiting local soldiers in India at a very early date. In 1772 the garrison of French India consisted of the "Pondichéry Regiment" (consisting of one battalion of white soldiers and one battalion of Cipahis or Sepoys) plus one company of naval artillery. During the

Left: Private of the Battalion of Cipahis with M1817 dress.

Right: Private of the Corps of Cipahis with M1908 khaki uniform.

American Revolution Great Britain and France again fought against each other in India and thus the French garrison of Pondichéry was notably expanded with the raising of four autonomous battalions of Cipahis (soon reduced to three) and of a single company of Indian volunteers who were commanded by French officers. With the end of the hostilities with Great Britain, the garrison of French India went back to its pre-war status. In August 1793, as part of the Revolutionary Wars, Pondichéry was attacked and conquered by the British who returned it to France only in 1802, following the signing of the Treaty of Amiens. Napoleon, at that time First Consul of France, tried to re-raise to Battalion of Cipahis and sent a military expedition to Pondichéry but when this arrived in 1803 hostilities with Great Britain had already resumed and thus the city could not be re-occupied by the French. The Congress of Vienna (1814–1815) returned Pondichéry to France, but the restored Bourbons, however, were not particularly interested in their only Indian colony and thus never attempted to raise any "white" military unit for garrisoning it. In 1817 the Battalion of Cipahis was reformed, with an overall strength of four companies. The corps, which could not serve outside India, mostly performed police duties and thus started to have a sort of "para-military" status. In 1867 the garrison of Pondichéry was reduced from four to two companies of Cipahis, each of the latter consisted of six French naval infantry officers, four Indian officers and 322 NCOs/privates. With the progression of time the Cipahis became an armed constabulary and thus in 1907 they became part of the French Gendarmerie (militarized police). From 1907 they also started to include a small mounted detachment, which mostly performed escort duties.

Indochina: native armies

Siam

Before the French colonized Indochina the four countries that made up the latter region of Asia – Siam (modern Thailand), Cambodia, Laos and Vietnam – all deployed sizeable military forces that had already been partly "modernized" along European lines. Since the second half of the 17th century the Kingdom of Siam was the dominant military power of Indochina and one of the most flourishing states of Asia. Two centuries later, by the time the French started to have growing colonial interests in Vietnam, the Kingdom of Siam still exerted a direct or indirect control over a good portion of Indochina – including Cambodia and Laos – but was experiencing a period of slow decline. During the reign of Napoleon III the French conquered a good portion of Vietnam and later transformed Cambodia into a protectorate. The Siamese had been the main regional rivals of Vietnam for centuries, but could not be happy of the arrival of the French military forces in Indochina. With the progression of time, in fact, it became apparent that the French government was interested in colonizing the whole region and thus Siam also risked being transformed into a protectorate. During the last decades of the 19th century tension started to grow between France and Siam, especially regarding possession of the Lao states. The latter had always been vassals of Siam but now the French wanted to absorb them in their sphere of influence. During this very difficult phase of its history, the Kingdom of Siam could count on the diplomatic and political support of Great Britain. The latter, in fact, controlled Burma and had a large border in common with Siam. The British were opposed to France's plans of transforming Siam into one of their protectorates, since they wanted to retain a "buffer zone" between their colonial possessions in Burma and the French ones in Indochina. Around 1890 the French started to put pressure on the Siamese government for obtaining permission to annex the Lao states located east of the Mekong River to their colonial possessions, claiming that those lands had always been under the control of Vietnam. The Siamese, counting on the support of Great Britain, refused to hand over the Lao provinces claimed by France and reinforced their military presence in the contested area.

In 1893, after some border incidents, the escalation of events led to the outbreak of hostilities between France and Siam. The French organized three military columns and invaded the Lao provinces of Siam from the east. Despite encountering some resistance, the French colonial troops were able to reach their objectives quite rapidly and to defeat the weak Siamese garrisons confronting them. After losing the contested territories, however, the Siamese government chose to not surrender to the French and to continue the war. The French responded by sending two of their warships to the Siamese capital of Bangkok, where an ultimatum was delivered to the Siamese government. Initially the latter tried to continue resisting, but after some of Bangkok's fortifications were bombarded by the French it decided to end any form of armed resistance. Following the end of the hostilities, a Franco-Siamese treaty was signed according to which Siam ceded all its Lao provinces to France and agreed to pay a large war indemnity. In addition, the Siamese were to de-militarize the western bank of the Mekong River that now marked the border between Siam and French Indochina. In 1896 France and Great Britain came to terms regarding their political differences in Indochina and signed an important international treaty, according to which the Kingdom of Siam was to remain independent and neutral for the years to come, in order to act as a "buffer state" located between the British and French territorial possessions. In practice, Siam became a protectorate ruled jointly by France and Great Britain. The latter, during the early years of the 20th century, annexed to their territorial possessions several border provinces that had always belonged to Siam during the previous decades. Until the early 1860s the Siamese Army remained a "traditional" Asian military force, having a militia-like organization and no modern firearms. Siam was an absolute monarchy and thus all the Siamese subjects were to perform military service when required to do so by the royal government. In theory all the able-bodied male subjects aged 18–60 could be called to serve in case of war, except for slaves, but in practice a series of social categories were completely exempt from compulsory military service (like members of the various ethnic minorities or Buddhist priests). This, combined with the fact that the recruiting officers could be corrupted quite easily by rich individuals who wanted to avoid military service, meant that in case of war mobilization the Siamese could rarely field more than 60,000 soldiers. The Siamese Army was a "militia-like" force, since its members were not professional fighters. They were armed with traditional weapons, had no training to speak of and could be mobilized only for the duration of a campaign. The various units were organized on "ad hoc" basis. They usually consisted of a "ban" or battalion of 1,000 men or of a "roy" or company of 100 men. Until the last decade of the 19th century, the Siamese Army comprised just one permanent corps made up of professional soldiers – the Royal Guard. The latter was organized on three autonomous branches, each of which performed different military functions. The first branch was the "*Dohar Na*" or "Front Soldiers Corps", consisting of soldiers who were chosen from the most loyal elements of the Siamese Army and was tasked with acting as the bodyguard of the king when the latter was in his palace. From many points of view the Front Soldiers Corps was a sort of "ceremonial" unit, since its members were still equipped with armour and spears like the Siamese soldiers of the 17th century. In practice, it was a corps of "palace guards" that was of no military use in case of war. It consisted of eight companies with 60 guardsmen each. The second branch of the Siamese Royal Guard was the "Second Guard", a corps tasked with protecting the king and the royal family when the latter were not in the royal palace. It consisted of three detachments (with two companies each) that were known as "inner", "main" and "outer". Each of the detachments comprised a "right company" and a "left company". The Second Guard also included the "*Sanam Dahar*" or "Amazon Guard", a company of female soldiers who were tasked with escorting the queen and with guarding the area of the royal palace inhabited by ladies. This small corps looked particularly "exotic" to the European observers of the time, who described its members as being dressed with Scottish kilts in imitation of the British Army's Highland units. The third branch of the Siamese Royal Guard was tasked with protecting the king while he was on campaign and thus was much more effective than the other two. It consisted of foreigners or Siamese individuals having foreign ancestry. In total this corps comprised around 3,000 soldiers, who could be members of the foreign communities living in Siam or mercenaries coming from abroad (mostly from Vietnam and Japan, according to contemporary sources). From the early 19th century the third branch of the Siamese Royal Guard also comprised a small corps equipped with modern firearms and wearing western-style uniforms. This was known as "Bayonetted-Rifles Guard" and consisted of 400 men. The latter were trained by foreign instructors, mostly ex-members of the East India Company's military forces. These British mercenary officers showed the men under their command how to maneuver and fire like the contemporary Indian Sepoys, but their efforts did not lead to great results. The Bayonetted-Rifles Guard was mostly recruited from Siam's small Christian communities or from individuals of mixed Siamese-Portuguese descent. It was equipped with old flintlock muskets and wore British-style red uniforms. The Siamese Army never included significant cavalry contingents, mostly because the few horses available on the Siamese territory were small ponies incapable of being employed in combat. In the 1880s the Siamese government tried to import some horses of good quality from Australia, but this project failed quite rapidly. As a result of the above, for long time the only mounted unit of the Siamese Army was the "Royal Horse Guards", consisting of a single "squadron" with around 60 men mounted on ponies. In 1870, as a result of the increasing need for new "westernized" military units, the pages of the Siamese monarch were militarized and were transformed into a new corps similar to the Bayonetted-Rifles Guard. The new unit, consisting of six companies with 92 men each, was given the denomination of "Faithful Royal Bodyguard" and was trained along British lines. During 1874–1881 the Siamese Royal Guard was completely reorganized and partly "westernized". The Front

Soldiers Guard was reorganized as an elite infantry regiment with the new denomination of "First Foot Guards" or "Palace Guard", while the other two branches of the Royal Guard were assembled together in order to form another infantry regiment known as "Second Foot Guard" or "Royal Guard". In 1895, following the defeat in the war with France, the Siamese government decided to reorganize its military forces along western lines and thus an early form of conscription was introduced. The whole territory of Siam was sub-divided into military areas and each of the latter was asked to provide a variable number of new conscripts every year. The latter were to perform compulsory military service for six months only and inside the borders of their own military circle. As a result they could continue living with their families for the whole year and working in the fields for half of the year. In 1905 a new form of conscription was introduced, according to which the period of compulsory military service lasted two years instead of six months. In 1905 the government organized two bodies of "reserve" military units: the First Reserve and the Second Reserve. After serving for two years in the active army, a Siamese soldier became part of the First Reserve and had to train for two months every year. After becoming older, the same individual entered the Second Reserve and had to train for just 15 days every year. At the beginning of the 20th century, despite the introduction of conscription, the Siamese Army was still quite small and consisted of the following regular units: the Palace Guard with two battalions of infantry, the Royal Guard with two battalions of infantry and one squadron of cavalry, three battalions of infantry with four companies each, one squadron of cavalry, one brigade of artillery and the Royal Marines Corps. The brigade of artillery had more or less the same establishment of an infantry battalion and was equipped with some modern Armstrong field guns plus a few Gatling machine guns. The Royal Marines, 2,000 in total, served on the ships of the royal family and on the few gunboats that made up the Siamese Navy. Around 1887 the Siamese government purchased 40,000 Snider-Enfield rifles from Great Britain, which remained the standard weapon of the Siamese Army until several thousands of new M1888 Mannlicher rifles produced in the Austro-Hungarian Empire were bought after 1893. With the introduction of conscription in 1895 the regular soldiers of the Siamese Army started to be dressed with a "westernized" uniform, consisting of just a few simple elements: soft visored cap, loose single-breasted jacket with folded collar and shoulder straps, trousers or "*panung*" kilt. All men served barefoot. During cold months the cap was dark blue with red bottom band and the jacket was dark blue with red collar, round cuffs and shoulder straps; during hot months the cap was white with dark blue bottom band and the jacket was white with dark blue collar, round cuffs and shoulder straps. The trousers were always white, but on most occasions they were substituted with a "*panung*" kilt of the same colour (the latter was part of Siam's national male costume). The officers were uniformed with white cork helmets and dark blue "patrol jackets" having black frogging on the front and black piping to the facings.

Cambodia and Laos

Until 1848 Cambodia was the main battleground for several conflicts that were fought between the two dominant regional military powers of Indochina, Siam and Vietnam. In the mid 19th century Cambodia started to experience a period of relative political autonomy, which ended in 1867 when the country became a French protectorate. France never transformed Cambodia, at least formally, into a colony but in practice the various Cambodian rulers who reigned after 1867 were little more than "puppet" monarchs. Cambodia was an absolute monarchy and thus all Cambodian subjects were to perform military service when required to do so by the royal government. In theory all the able-bodied male subjects aged 18–50 could be called to serve in case of war, except for the slaves. In practice, however, a series of social categories were completely exempt from compulsory military service. This, combined with the fact that Cambodia had a quite small population, meant that in case of war mobilization the Cambodians could not field more than 30,000 soldiers. The Cambodian Army was a "militia-like" force, since its members were not professional fighters. They were armed with traditional weapons, had no training to speak of and could be mobilized only for the duration of a campaign. To supplement their standard military forces, quite frequently the Cambodian monarchs recruited contingents of mercenaries from Malaya or the Philippines. The recruiting of mercenaries was financed with the fines that the central government was paid by its subjects for each slave or ill man who could not be called to serve in the royal army. The latter comprised no formal units because it always retained a "temporary" nature. The government was expected to provide weapons and supplies to the mobilized military contingents, but this happened quite rarely. Cambodia's military forces, however, also comprised a small permanent Royal Guard that consisted of regular professional soldiers who were under the direct orders of the monarch and acted as the latter's bodyguard. The Cambodian Royal Guard consisted of 12 companies with 50 or 60 men each, some of whom were mercenaries coming from Malaya or the Philippines. Each of these companies, in time of peace, served a month at a time in rotation and provided the garrison for the royal palace. In case of war mobilization, all the soldiers of the Royal Guard were called to serve. After Cambodia became a French protectorate, in 1874 the Royal Guard was given French-style uniforms and was re-trained by French military instructors. After being reorganized by the French, the small Cambodian Royal Guard, mustering around 1,000 soldiers, came to comprise sub-units of infantry, cavalry and artillery.

Laos was fragmented into a series of "petty kingdoms" since the early 18th century and thus was the weakest of the four Indochinese states. During the first half of the 19th century the various Lao realms were either Siamese or Vietnamese protectorates. After Vietnam was conquered by the French, Laos became a puppet state of Siam. In 1888, after a brief diplomatic and military confrontation between France and Siam, the territory of Laos became a French protectorate. France never transformed Laos, at least formally, into a colony but in practice the various Lao rulers who reigned after 1888 were little more than "puppet" monarchs. Each Lao state had its own hereditary monarch, who exerted absolute power over his subjects. The latter, in case of war, could be called to serve at the orders of their tribal chieftains. Unlike what happened in Cambodia the "militia-like" forces of the Lao states were raised on a tribal basis. No permanent military contingents existed and thus the mobilized men could be called to serve only for the duration of a campaign. The various Lao rulers were to provide supplies to their soldiers in time of war, but they did so quite rarely. As in Cambodia a series of social categories, including slaves, were completely exempt from military service. This, combined with the fact that the various Lao states had very small populations, meant that the military capabilities of Laos were extremely limited. In time of war the largest Lao realms could deploy around 5,000 soldiers each. The latter were not professional fighters, were armed with traditional weapons and had no training to speak of. The Lao rulers, however, also deployed some small "standing" military forces having a professional and permanent nature. These acted as "royal bodyguards" and with time started to be partly "westernized" by being given European-style uniforms and modern weapons. During 1895, in the largest Lao state of Luang Prabang, a few French military instructors reformed the local royal bodyguard that was already equipped with modern rifles since the early 1890s.

Vietnam

The French colonization of Vietnam was a long and difficult process, which lasted for several decades. Everything began in 1857, when two Spanish Catholic missionaries were executed in Vietnam following a direct order from the local monarch (who was, at least formally, a vassal king of the Chinese Qing Empire). Napoleon III, who had already deployed a sizeable French expeditionary force in the Far East to fight in the Second Opium War against China, saw this event as a perfect "casus belli" for an intervention against the Kingdom of Vietnam. He ordered to his troops deployed in China to attack southern Vietnam, with the idea of launching a punitive expedition that would transform the Kingdom of Vietnam into a French protectorate. The campaign was conducted together with Spain, which provided a large military contingent, mostly coming from the Spanish colony of the Philippines. The hostilities began in September 1858 and were conducted in the southern region of Vietnam, called Cochinchina by the French. The westerners landed at Da Nang and conquered it, but were soon besieged in the latter city by the Vietnamese Army. For several months the Franco-Spanish forces were blocked in Da Nang and thus could not make any progress in further conquest of Cochinchina. Meanwhile, in 1859 a Franco-Spanish token force attacked the important city of Saigon by moving along the Mekong River. After some harsh fighting the urban centre was occupied by the westerners, but in 1860 the Franco-Spanish forces were obliged to evacuate Da Nang and were besieged inside Saigon. In 1861 Napoleon III sent massive reinforcements to Cochinchina and thanks to the latter Saigon was freed from the Vietnamese forces besieging it. The year continued with a series of Franco-Spanish victories and with the progressive French conquest of Cochinchina's provinces. In 1862, with the signing of the Treaty of Saigon, the hostilities came to an end. The Kingdom of Vietnam was forced to cede Cochinchina to the French, to open the Mekong River to French military and merchant ships, to pay a large war indemnity to France and Spain and to permit the free practice of the Catholic faith on Vietnamese soil. In 1867 another three Vietnamese provinces were added to the newly-established French colony of Cochinchina and thus the French started to have complete control over the Mekong River's large delta.

After the events of 1858–1867 Vietnam became increasingly weaker from a military point of view and came under an increasingly strong Chinese political influence. The Vietnamese, in fact, considered the Qing Empire as the only state that could help them in preserving their independence from France's colonial ambitions. In the summer of 1873 the French led an expedition against Hanoi, the capital of the Kingdom of Vietnam, with the objective of transforming what remained of the latter country (the central region of Annam and the northern region of Tonkin) into a protectorate. The expedition, however, was a complete failure since the Vietnamese could count on the support of one of China's strongest warlords, Liu Yongfu, who commanded the so-called "Black Flag Army". The latter attacked the French in Hanoi and killed their commander. In 1882 the French attempted again to conquer central and northern Vietnam, this time by assembling a very large military force. Hanoi was occupied quite easily, but during the years 1883–1884 the hostilities continued with increasing violence due to the strong resistance organized by the Vietnamese. In the summer of 1884 Qing China decided to intervene in the ongoing conflict on Vietnam's side, since the Chinese considered northern and central Vietnam as part of their sphere of influence. Again time the Black Flag Army fought with distinction, together with the other Chinese military forces, but in the end the Qing Empire was obliged to abandon Vietnam to its destiny in the spring of 1885, after the French attacked with substantial military forces the large Chinese island of Formosa (modern Taiwan). After the Chinese troops left Vietnam the hostilities lasted for another year and ended with the final defeat of the Vietnamese. Annam and Tonkin, in fact, were split into two autonomous political entities and transformed into French protectorates. On 17 October 1887 Cochinchina, Annam and Tonkin were assembled together into the new and larger colony of French Indochina (which also comprised the Protectorate of Cambodia and later came to include Laos).

During the first half of the 19th century the Vietnamese Army consisted of two main components: the "*Linh Ve*" or central standing army and the "*Linh Co*" or provincial armies. The *Linh Ve* included a large and strong Royal Guard or "*Kinh Binh*", which consisted of 12,000 elite soldiers assembled into three infantry regiments with four battalions each. The line units of the *Linh Ve* consisted of 40 infantry regiments, which were assembled into five brigades having eight regiments each and bearing the following denominations: Advance Guard Brigade, Centre Brigade, Right Wing Brigade, Left Wing Brigade and Rear Guard Brigade. Each regiment comprised two battalions and a single battalion had five or six companies mustering 50 soldiers each. The 40 regiments described above were armed with antiquated firearms and were trained according to contemporary Chinese models. They were supplemented by another 40 regiments, always part of the *Linh Ve*, which had a similar internal organization but were equipped with traditional weapons like spears and bows. The *Linh Co* was a sort of "auxiliary army" recruited on a territorial basis. Each of the Vietnamese provinces, in fact, was to mobilize an infantry brigade with five regiments of such troops in case of war. In peacetime the *Linh Co* was a sedentary militia acting as the police force of the various provinces. The provincial forces were commanded by the mandarins, royal officials who played a prominent role in the administrative system of Vietnam. The Vietnamese Army also comprised soldiers provided by the "*Don Dien*" or "military colonies", the latter being military settlements established in some strategic areas of Vietnam that were inhabited farmers/soldiers who, in exchange for their military services, were given a plot of land. The *Don Dien* were mostly located along the south-western border of Vietnam and were well fortified. As a result, they acted as a sort of "line of defence" for the nearby frontier. The *Don Dien* soldiers were assembled into 24 infantry regiments with ten companies each, organized on a canton basis and mostly performing garrison duties. The Vietnamese Army did not include separate artillery regiments, since the artillery pieces were attached to the various infantry units according to traditional Chinese practice. No cavalry corps were part of the Vietnamese Army, except for a single squadron mounted on ponies that was part of the Royal Guard. Vietnam had a strong navy, which was organized in 30 regiments having the same internal structure as the army ones. The members of such regiments were mostly recruited from the coastal provinces of the country. Six units consisted of naval infantry, while the remaining ones consisted of seamen and each of them was garrisoned in one of Vietnam's 24 major ports.

Indochina: colonial troops

The French raised their first native troops in Vietnam in February 1859, during the campaign that led to the conquest of Cochinchina. These consisted of two infantry companies, mostly recruited from Christian Vietnamese who took refuge in the city of Da Nang that was occupied by the Franco-Spanish forces. In March of 1861 the number of companies was increased to four and during 1862 these were consolidated into a single "Native Battalion". This, however, was quite short-lived and was soon reduced to a single company with 235 men in 1863. During 1870–1871 a small platoon of mounted guides was temporarily added to the Native Company, the latter finally disbanded in April 1876. In 1862 the French also raised a militia corps from the inhabitants of Cochinchina who were loyal to them. This para-military police force was known as "*Corps de Matas*" and consisted of 600 men (mostly recruited from Saigon). In 1877, however, the corps was disbanded. On 2 December 1879 the French colonial authorities in Vietnam decided that the time had come for the formation of some larger native military corps. As a result, the new "*Annamite Tirailleurs*" were created. Initially this consisted of just two infantry battalions with 250 men each (mostly former members of the *Corps de Matas)*, which were soon increased to three. Annam was a term used in Europe to identify the central portion of Vietnam, but the early Annamite Tirailleurs were all recruited from Cochinchina. The new battalions took part to the conquest of Annam and Tonkin, during which their members fought with great courage against the Chinese troops and showed to be excellent light infantrymen under the guidance of their French officers and NCOs. On 1 June 1907 the three battalions were consolidated into the 1st Regiment of Annamite Tirailleurs and a 2nd Regiment of Annamite Tirailleurs was created. In 1880 the French raised their first native troops from central and northern Vietnam, consisting of ten infantry companies. These performed well during the military operations of 1883 and thus in 1884 were used as cadres for the formation of two regiments of "Tonkinese Tirailleurs". The latter had three battalions with four companies of 252 men each. In 1885 the number of battalions in each regiment was increased to four. Due to the success of the first two units during the campaigns that led to the French conquest of Annam and Tonkin, a 3rd Regiment of Tonkinese Tirailleurs (1885) and a 4th Regiment of Tonkinese Tirailleurs (1886) were created. The Tonkinese Tirailleurs performed very well against the bands of bandits and Chinese irregulars who infested Tonkin until 1896. During 1890–1898 the 4th Regiment of Tonkinese Tirailleurs was temporarily disbanded, but in 1902 a new 5th Regiment of Tonkinese Tirailleurs was formed, to provide the garrison for the "Leased Territory of Guangzhouwan" (a small French colonial enclave located on the southern coast of China near the island of Hainan).

On 4 August 1899, to protect the northern frontier of Indochina from the incursions of the bandits and of the irregular troops active in southern China, the French raised a first infantry company from the local communities living

Private of the Annamite Tirailleurs with M1885 dress. ASKB

in northern Tonkin. The members of the unit were known as "Chinese Tirailleurs". On 20 June 1902 the corps was reorganized as a battalion with two companies and assumed the new denomination of "Frontier Tirailleurs". Despite its original name, the unit was not recruited from Chinese individuals living in northern Tonkin but from the "*montagnard*" or "mountaineer" tribes of northern Tonkin. The latter had strong anti-Chinese feelings and a perfect knowledge of their home territories. The Frontier Tirailleurs performed very well against the Chinese bandits who penetrated across the northern border of Vietnam, but were disbanded in 1907 when the frontier areas were fully pacified. Most of the former members of the corps were absorbed into the 2nd Regiment of Tonkinese Tirailleurs. On 28 May 1902 the French organized their first native units in the protectorate of Cambodia. Known as "Cambodian Tirailleurs", this consisted of two infantry companies recruited from the Khmer population. The corps mostly acted as a "constabulary corps" tasked with fighting against the many bands of bandits active in the Cambodian countryside. It was disbanded in 1907 and most of its members were absorbed into the 1st Regiment of Annamite Tirailleurs. In 1885 the Vietnamese Army was completely disbanded after having been defeated by the French. The latter, however, retained in place some form of "puppet" native government that was given some

NCO of the Annamite Tirailleurs wearing M1885 dress.

Private of the Annamite Tirailleurs with M1885 uniform, including the peculiar "salacco" round and flat hat made of bamboo.

Private of the Tonkinese Tirailleurs wearing M1885 uniform.

small military forces despite being completely subservient to the colonial authorities. The new "Vietnamese Army" was reorganized in May 1886 by a French military mission. It was to comprise four light infantry battalions, known as "Annamite Chasseurs". Each battalion consisted of 710 soldiers, including 57 French officers and NCOs. The four units were paid by the puppet Vietnamese government and one of them (the 4th Battalion) acted as the guard of the monarch. In January 1890 the Annamite Chasseurs were disbanded and their members were absorbed into the para-military Native Civil Guard of Annam and Tonkin. The regular native military forces raised by the French in Indochina also comprised some units of cavalry and artillery. During 1862–1871 a short-lived "Squadron of Cochinchinese Spahis" was in existence and performed auxiliary duties like conducting reconnaissance missions. During 1883–1885, for the military campaigns in Annam and Tonkin, a temporary squadron of lancers was created. In the years 1883–1899 there also was a single platoon of "Tonkinese Spahis". Soon after the latter was disbanded, the French formed a new cavalry squadron, known as "Annamite Mounted Chasseurs", that was recruited from the best elements of the Annamite Tirailleurs and was commanded by French officers. This unit served quite well but was disbanded in 1908. After the latter year a single platoon of Vietnamese cavalry was retained in service by the French, mostly employed for parades and other ceremonies. On 12 February 1899 the French organized 14 artillery batteries with mixed French and Vietnamese personnel, which were stationed in various areas of Indochina and performed very well. These were supported by a single squadron of Vietnamese artillery drivers, which had been raised in 1868. On 5 November 1904 the French also created two companies of pioneers and pontoon-handlers, having 124 men each (one for Cochinchina and one for Tonkin) that were employed to perform public works.

The regular native units of Indochina described above were supplemented by a series of para-military corps that were progressively raised by the French. On 18 February 1862 the colonial authorities organized a militia in Cochinchina, which was to consist of two foot companies for each of the provinces that were under French control. Tasked with the defence of the villages located in the countryside, the "Militia of Cochinchina" was gradually expanded and came to comprise 5,000 men by 1880 when it was disbanded and absorbed into the new "Native Civil Guard of Cochinchina". This, consisting of 3,268 men, existed until January 1886 when it was replaced by a new para-military corps that was made up of former members of the Annamite Tirailleurs. The new unit included a mounted detachment tasked with guarding the railways, armed with lances. On 19 September 1909 this para-military corps of veterans was disbanded and was replaced by the new "Civil Guard of Local Police". The latter consisted of 700 policemen and had cadres provided by the French gendarmerie. Its members were mostly former members of the Annamite Tirailleurs. In time of peace the Civil Guard of Local Police was stationed in the major urban centres, while in time of war it was to act as a sort of "military police". On 19 July 1888, following the example of the Native Civil Guard of Cochinchina, a similar corps, known as "Native Civil Guard of Annam and Tonkin", was created by the French in central and northern Vietnam. The new para-military organization was formed from a small militia corps that had already been created by the French in

Private of the Tonkinese Tirailleurs with M1885 dress.

Privates of the Tonkinese Tirailleurs around 1890.

Private of the Tonkinese Tirailleurs with khaki-brown campaign dress. Note the white cover worn over the "salacco" hat.

Private of the Chinese Tirailleurs.

Annam during 1886. The Native Civil Guard of Annam and Tonkin was structured in two autonomous branches: one for Annam with 9 "brigades" and one for Tonkin with 14 "brigades". A single brigade consisted of around 300 policemen. The brigades of Tonkin were supplemented by a semi-autonomous "Railroad Guard" that deployed a total of 1,200 men. Like Cochinchina, Annam and Tonkin, the French protectorates of Cambodia and Laos also had their own corps of Native Civil Guard. The "Native Civil Guard of Cambodia" was created on 11 July 1903 and gradually came to comprise 2,500 men. From a formal point of view, it was at the orders of the Cambodian monarchs. The "Native Civil Guard of Laos" was raised in May 1894 following the Franco-Siamese War and gradually came to comprise 1,700 men.

Private of the Cambodian Tirailleurs.

Private of the Native Civil Guard of Annam and Tonkin around 1890. ASKB

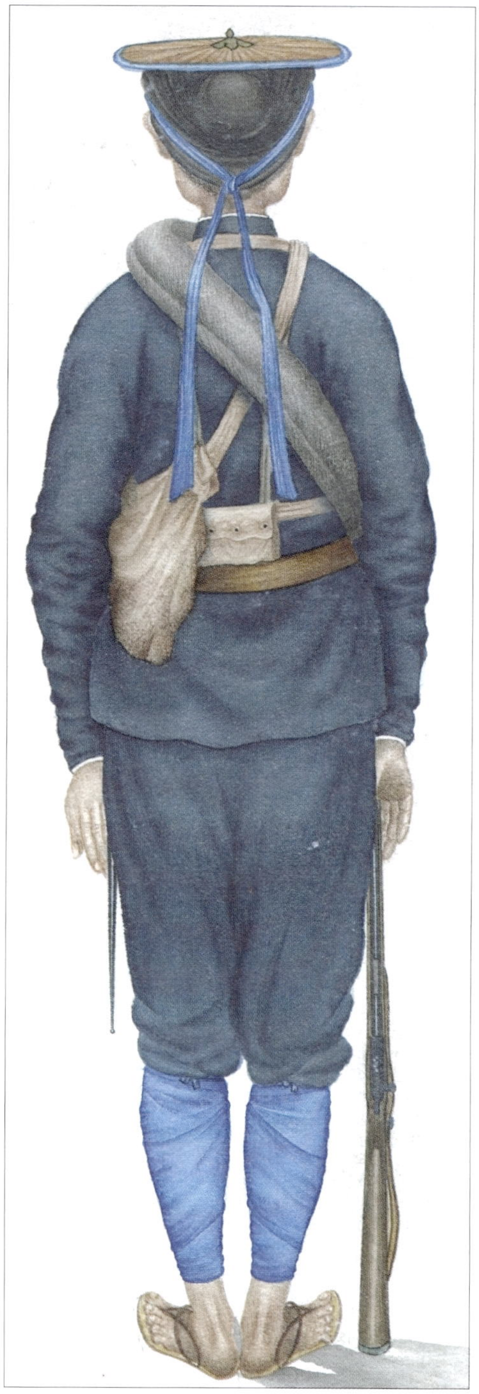

Private of the Native Civil Guard of Annam and Tonkin around 1890. ASKB

Uniforms and weapons

Senegalese Spahis

Initially the Senegalese Spahis were dressed exactly like the Algerian ones, except for the headgear since they wore the red *chéchia* without turban. The *tombò* of the Senegalese Spahis was light blue like that of the 1st Regiment of Algerian Spahis. In 1862, for campaign use, the Senegalese Spahis were given wide-brimmed straw hats and in 1878 the standard headgear of the corps became a white tropical helmet made of cork having a brass star-and-crescent badge on the front. In 1879 the original "Algerian" uniform was replaced by a much more practical one, which remained in service until 1914. This consisted of the M1878 tropical helmet and a single-breasted red jacket having pointed cuffs piped in yellow and collar patches bearing the same badge as the helmet embroidered in yellow. The new uniform was completed by a red waist-sash and by baggy light blue trousers. During hot months a white version of the jacket and the trousers was worn. The uniforms of the Senegalese Spahis' officers followed the same evolution of those worn by the Algerian Spahis' officers. The saddles and weapons employed by the Senegalese Spahis were the same used by the Algerian Spahis.

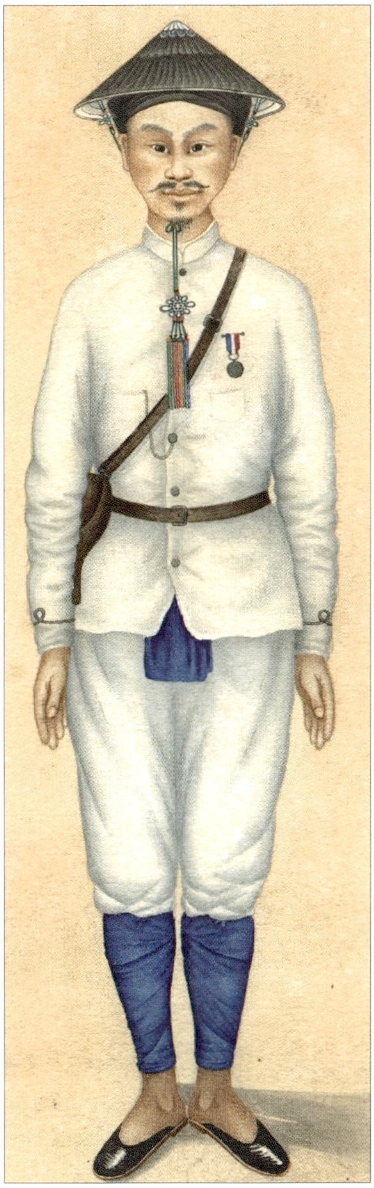

Left: Officer of the Native Civil Guard of Annam and Tonkin in 1890, with white summer dress. ASKB

Right: Private of the Native Civil Guard of Annam and Tonkin in 1900, with khaki campaign dress. ASKB

Sudanese Spahis

Uniformed and equipped like the Senegalese Spahis.

Senegalese Tirailleurs

Upon their formation in 1857 the Senegalese Tirailleurs were given a "Zouave-style" dress that was richly ornamented. It consisted of the following elements: red *chéchia* with light blue tassel and white turban, dark blue *veste* with yellow trimming on the edges, yellow piping to the pointed cuffs and yellow S-shaped knot embroidered on each side, dark blue *sédria* waistcoat with yellow piping around the neck and on the front, dark blue loose trousers with yellow decorative embroiderings on the sides, red waist-sash, black spats and black shoes. The native officers were uniformed like their men but the tassel of their *chéchia* was golden and both their *veste* and *sédria* were richly laced and embroidered with gold. In 1889 the colour of the native officers' dress was changed from dark blue to light blue. In 1898 a completely new uniform was introduced for them, which comprised a dark blue patrol jacket with black edging and frogging that was worn together with dark blue trousers having yellow side-stripe. In 1868 the Senegalese Tirailleurs were given a new campaign dress, consisting of a dark blue single-breasted and collarless jacket. This had yellow piping around the neck and on the pointed cuffs. In 1873 the new campaign jacket was adopted as the standard dress of the Senegalese Tirailleurs together with straight-cut dark blue trousers having yellow side-stripe and red *chéchia* without turban. In 1876, however, the pre-1873 dress was restored as required by the Senegalese infantrymen. In 1889 the "Zouave-style" uniform was finally abolished and replaced by the M1868 campaign dress. From 1889 the latter started to be also produced in a khaki version, which was worn on campaign while the original M1868 uniform was used on parade. Both the M1889 dark blue and M1889 khaki dress had dark blue collar patches with the letters "TS" embroidered in red. The footwear of the Senegalese Tirailleurs consisted of simple sandals, but khaki puttees worn together with black shoes became increasingly popular.

Sudanese Tirailleurs

Uniformed and equipped like the Senegalese Tirailleurs.

Native Gendarmes of Senegal

The uniform of this corps was very similar to that worn by the Senegalese Spahis until 1879. It consisted of red *chéchia* with light blue tassel and white turban, red *veste* with black trimming on the edges, black piping to the light blue pointed cuffs and black S-shaped knot embroidered on each side, light blue *sédria* waistcoat with black piping around the neck and on the front, light blue waist-sash, dark blue loose trousers, light blue cloak and brown leather boots.

Hausa Tirailleurs

This unit was given the M1868 campaign uniform of the Senegalese Tirailleurs, but with some peculiarities – a brass star badge placed on the front of the red *chéchia*, four stripes of yellow frogging ending in trefoils on the front of the jacket and yellow "shoulder cords". In 1892 these peculiar elements were abolished.

Native Civil Guard of Dahomey

The dress of this para-military corps was very similar to that worn by the Senegalese Tirailleurs upon their formation and thus was "Zouave-style". It consisted of the following elements: red *chéchia* with medium blue tassel and brass badge on the front (consisting of a crescent and a star), dark blue *veste* with green trimming on the edges, green piping to the dark blue pointed cuffs and green S-shaped knot embroidered on each side, dark blue *sédria* waistcoat with green piping around the neck and on the front, light blue waist-sash and red loose trousers.

Native Civil Guard of the Ivory Coast

Uniformed and equipped like the Senegalese Tirailleurs.

Gabonese Tirailleurs

Uniformed and equipped like the Senegalese Tirailleurs.

Battalion of Guinea

Uniformed and equipped like the Senegalese Tirailleurs.

Native Infantry Regiment of Congo

Uniformed and equipped like the Senegalese Tirailleurs.

Native Battalion of Chari and Mixed Battalion of Tchad

Uniformed and equipped like the Senegalese Tirailleurs.

Territorial Battalions of Tirailleurs

Uniformed and equipped like the Senegalese Tirailleurs.

Méharistes

Uniformed and equipped like the Algerian Méharistes.

Native Guard Brigade of Somaliland

This corps had the same khaki campaign uniform as the Senegalese Tirailleurs and wore it with a red *chéchia*.

Sakalava Tirailleurs

The original uniform of this unit was very simple. It consisted of the following elements: red *chéchia* with medium blue tassel, dark blue single-breasted jacket with red collar and pointed cuffs, white straight trousers. In 1887 this was replaced by a new dress, very similar to the uniform worn by the soldiers of the Hova Army: medium blue visorless round cap with red bottom band, medium blue single-breasted jacket with red collar and round cuffs, red shoulder straps, white straight trousers. The collar had dark blue patches with a letter "S" embroidered in red.

Malagasy Tirailleurs

Uniformed and equipped like the Senegalese Tirailleurs, but with red as facing colour instead of yellow.

Isle-de-Bourbon's Militia

This corps, re-organized following the restoration of the Bourbons, had a very simple but practical uniform. It consisted of the following elements: black round hat with white cockade having lace holder of the same colour and white plume, white single-breasted coat with dark blue collar and round cuffs, white trousers and white gaiters. The various units were distinguishable by the colour of their fringed epaulettes: red for grenadiers and artillerymen, green for chasseurs and cavalrymen. The fusiliers had simple white shoulder straps piped in dark blue.

Volunteers of La Réunion

Uniformed and equipped like the Naval Infantry.

Company of Cayenne's Black Chasseurs

This company of black light infantrymen was issued with some sort of "uniform" only in 1831. Their simple dress consisted of dark blue *toque* soft cap, dark blue blouse with red shoulder straps and dark blue trousers.

Cipahis of India

In 1817 the Sepoys in French service were given a simple dress that was quite similar to that worn by their predecessors of the 18th century. It consisted of the following elements: white round and flat turban with red edging, emerald green short-tailed coat with red collar and pointed cuffs, red frontal plastron and fringed "epaulettes", light blue waist-sash and white short trousers (*jangheas*) trimmed with red lace. Under Napoleon III the Cipahis were issued a new "Zouave-style" uniform: red *chéchia* with medium blue tassel and white turban having red stripes, dark blue *veste* with red trimming on the edges, red piping to the dark blue pointed cuffs and red S-shaped knot embroidered on each side, dark blue *sédria* waistcoat with red piping around the neck and on the front, tricolour waist-sash and dark blue loose trousers. In 1884 the dress described above was modified: the turban was removed from the headgear, dark blue "shoulder wings" were added to the *veste*, the pointed cuffs became red, the waistcoat became red with black piping and the trousers became red with black piping on the sides. In 1908 a new khaki uniform was introduced: dark blue *chéchia* with red tassel, khaki single-breasted jacket with red piping to collar and pointed cuffs, khaki loose trousers and white spats. The small mounted detachment wore a peculiar dress: dark blue *chéchia* with red tassel, dark blue single-breasted jacket with red piping to front, collar and round cuffs, red cuff flaps, white shoulder cords and "aiguillette", light blue trousers with dark blue side-stripe and black leather boots.

Native Battalion of Cochinchina

The uniform of this unit was very simple and was based on the local "national" costume of southern Vietnam. It comprised the following elements: *salacco* round and flat hat made of bamboo worn over a black turban confining the hair, dark blue single-breasted jacket with red pointed cuffs, dark blue loose trousers (white during hot months) and red waist-sash.

Corps de Matas

The dress of this corps was very similar to that of the Native Battalion of Cochinchina. It consisted of the following elements:

salacco hat worn over a red turban confining the hair, dark blue single-breasted jacket with red trimming on the external edges and red pointed cuffs, white loose trousers and red waist-sash.

Annamite Tirailleurs

The uniform of the Annamite Tirailleurs consisted of just a few elements but soon became iconic in French Indochina. It was as follows: *salacco* hat worn over a red turban confining the hair, dark blue single-breasted jacket with red trimming on the external edges and red piping to both standing collar and pointed cuffs, dark blue loose trousers (white during summer) and red waist-sash. For some time light blue collar patches bearing the company number embroidered in red were used. Each soldier of the Annamite Tirailleurs also received an entirely white and an entirely black version of this dress. The first was worn during hot months, the second was used as fatigue dress. From 1896 the corps was issued an entirely brownish khaki version, which was to be worn on campaign. The Annamite Tirailleurs, like all the native soldiers recruited by the French in Indochina, served with their traditional sandals.

Tonkinese Tirailleurs

The first uniform issued to the Tonkinese Tirailleurs was quite different from that worn by the Annamite Tirailleurs. It was as follows: conical-shaped hat made of bamboo and painted with three horizontal bands in the colours of France's flag worn over a red turban confining the hair, white single-breasted jacket with red trimming on the external edges and red round cuffs, dark blue loose trousers and red waist-sash. On the chest the jacket had a white badge with the company number embroidered in dark blue. From 1886 the Tonkinese Tirailleurs were given the same uniforms and equipment as the Annamite Tirailleurs.

Chinese Tirailleurs

Initially this corps was given a "Chinese-style" dress, which was not particularly loved by its Vietnamese members. It consisted of the following elements: *salacco* hat worn over a red turban confining the hair, dark blue "Chinese-style" coat with yellow trimming on the external edges and a yellow disk on the chest bearing red Chinese characters, white loose trousers. The unit was later issued the same uniform as the Tonkinese Tirailleurs, but without the red turban and red waist-sash. The "montagnard" soldiers of this corps had long pigtails, like most of the contemporary Chinese soldiers.

Cambodian Tirailleurs

The Cambodian Tirailleurs wore a simple but quite distinctive uniform. This consisted of the following elements: wide-brimmed straw hat having a red band wrapped around its main body, dark blue single-breasted jacket with red piping to standing collar and pointed cuffs, red waist-sash and dark blue tight trousers with red side-stripe. An entirely white version of this dress was worn during hot months. On parade the straw hat was replaced with a red soft *basque*.

Annamite Chasseurs

This corps was uniformed and equipped like the Annamite Tirailleurs, but the jacket of its dress was brownish khaki instead of dark blue.

French Indochina's cavalry and artillery

The Squadron of Cochinchinese Spahis and the Platoon of Tonkinese Spahis were uniformed like the Senegalese Spahis but with a white *salacco* as headgear. The Annamite Mounted Chasseurs, instead, were dressed like the Annamite Tirailleurs. The cavalry corps formed in 1908 wore white *salacco*, dark blue single-breasted jacket with red collar and dark blue collar patches bearing a red flaming grenade embroidered in red, dark blue trousers with red side-stripe. The artillery batteries organized in 1899 had white *salacco*, dark blue single-breasted jacket with red collar patches bearing a flaming grenade embroidered in dark blue, dark blue trousers with red double side-stripe.

Cochinchina's Militia

The original uniform of the corps consisted of *salacco*, dark blue single-breasted jacket with pointed cuffs in the distinctive colour of each province and white loose trousers. In 1877 the *salacco* was replaced with the same conical hat worn by the early Tonkinese Tirailleurs and each militiaman was given a black turban for his hair.

Native Civil Guard of Cochinchina

The dress of this para-military corps consisted of *salacco* trimmed in light blue and worn with black turban for the hair, entirely dark blue single-breasted jacket, light blue waist-sash and dark blue loose trousers. An entirely white version of this uniform was worn during hot months and from 1896 a new entirely khaki version was introduced for campaign use.

Civil Guard of Local Police

Uniformed and equipped like the Annamite Tirailleurs.

Native Civil Guard of Annam and Tonkin

Uniformed and equipped like the Native Civil Guard of Cochinchina.

Native Civil Guard of Cambodia

Uniformed and equipped like the Native Civil Guard of Cochinchina, but with the same red *basque* of the Cambodian Tirailleurs as headgear.

Native Civil Guard of Laos

Uniformed and equipped like the Native Civil Guard of Cochinchina, but with the same straw hat (having light blue band) of the Cambodian Tirailleurs as headgear.

Select bibliography

Abbott, Peter, *Rivals of the Raj: Non-British Colonial Armies in Asia 1497-1941*, Foundry Books, 2010
Augarde, Jacques, *La longue route des Tabors*, Editions France Empire, 1983
Busson, Jean, *Yusuf: Prince des Spahis*, Editions Le Triomphe, 2016
Chartrand, René, *French Naval & Colonial Troops*, Osprey Publishing, 2018
Deroo, Eric, *Héros de Tunisie*, Ceres Production, 2005
Devautour P. and Huré R., *L'Armée d'Afrique 1830-1962*, Lavauzelle, 1980
Glogowski P. and de Gmeline P., *Histoire des Spahis 1834-1918*, Editions Le Triomphe, 2018
Heath, Ian, *Armies of the Nineteenth Century in Asia: Burma and Indo-China*, Foundry Books, 2003
Humbert, G., *Madagascar: L'Ile et ses habitants*, Berger-Levrault Editeurs, 1895
Jouineau, André, *L'Armée de Napoleon III*, Editions Heimdal, 2018
Jouineau, André, *L'Armée Française de 1914*, Histoire et Collections, 2014
La Sabretache, *L'Expédition d'Afrique Mai-Juillet 1830*, Carnets de La Sabretache, 1981
La Sabretache, *Les Chasseurs d'Afrique 1831-1964*, Carnets de La Sabretache, 1974
La Sabretache, *Les Joyeux*, Carnets de La Sabretache, 1979
La Sabretache, *Les Spahis*, Carnets de La Sabretache, 1982
La Sabretache, *Les Troupes de Marine 1622-1900*, Carnets de La Sabretache, 1987
La Sabretache, *Les Zouaves*, Carnets de La Sabretache, 1985
La Sabretache, *Tirailleurs Algériens et Tunisiens 1830-1964*, Carnets de La Sabretache, 1980
Montagnon, Pierre, *L'Armée d'Afrique*, Pygmalion, 2012
Rosière, Pierre, *Spahis*, Richer/Vilo, 1984
Sicard J. and Vauvillier F., *Les Chasseurs d'Afrique*, Histoire et Collections, 2008
Vv.Aa., *Histoire et épopée des Troupes Coloniales*, Les Presses Modernes, 1956
Vv.Aa., *Historique de l'Artillerie de la Marine*, Dumoulin, 1889
Windrow, Martin, *French Foreign Legion 1831-1871*, Osprey Publishing, 2016
Windrow, Martin, *French Foreign Legion 1872-1914*, Osprey Publishing, 2010
Windrow, Martin, *French Foreign Legionnaire 1890-1914*, Osprey Publishing, 2011